Wang Ruowang

HUNGER TRILOGY

Wang Ruowang

HUNGER TRILOGY

Translated by Kyna Rubin
with Ira Kasoff
Introduction by Kyna Rubin

An East Gate Book

M.E. Sharpe, Inc.

Armonk, New York
London, England

An East Gate Book

Copyright © 1991 by M. E. Sharpe, Inc.

Available in the United Kingdom and Europe from M. E. Sharpe,
Publishers, 3 Henrietta Street, London WC2E 8LU.

Library of Congress Cataloging-in-Publication Data

Wang, Jo-wang.
    [Chi o san pu ch'ü. English]
    Hunger trilogy / by Wang Ruowang ; translators, Kyna Rubin with
Ira Kasoff : introduction by Kyna Rubin.
      p.   cm.
    Translation of : Chi o san pu ch'ü.
    Includes bibliographical references.
    ISBN 0-87332-739-X
    I. Rubin, Kyna.   II. Kasoff, Ira E.   III. Title.
PL2919.J6C3813
895.1′352—dc20
                                                91–9017
                                                CIP

Printed in the United States of America

MV   10 9 8 7 6 5 4 3 2 1

To Wang Ruowang

*Who has always outshined his jailers
through his dignity, wit, and persistence.
May these gifts help you now.*

Contents

Translator's Note

THIS English translation is based on the original Chinese text, *Ji'e sanbuqu*, which appeared in *Shouhuo*, 1980, 1: 116–73. People's Literature Publishing House (Renmin wenxue chubanshe) subsequently reprinted the Chinese text in a 1983 collection of Wang Ruowang's fiction entitled *Yanbuzhu de guangmang* (The indistinguishable light). This version is not the same as the original and contains omissions of several passages that were politically sensitive at the time of printing. In 1984 East-West Culture Publishing Company in Hong Kong published another reprint entitled *Guogong heiyu neimu* (Inside the dark prisons of the KMT and CCP). This edition is based on the already edited version in *Yanbuzhu de guangmang*, but it goes a step further by adding subtitles not in the author's original text. This version also contains inaccuracies in Han Shanbi's introduction about the author and the characters in the book.

I would like to express my deep appreciation to Timothy Cheek, Howard Goldblatt, Wu Dawei, Madelyn Ross, and Leo Ou-fan Lee for their support and guidance.

K.R.

KYNA RUBIN

Introduction: The Growth of a Nation and an Intellectual

THE TIME was 1988—more than twenty years since the events described in part 3 of *Hunger Trilogy*. Three cellmates of two decades earlier, a writer, a businessman, and a ship captain, older men now, but each in his own way enjoying the fruits of the economic and cultural liberalization of the 1980s, sat around a small table in one of their homes drinking and laughing good-naturedly about the fate that brought them together to experience hunger in a dark corner of Shanghai in the late 1960s. "Here they are, all the 'cow-devils and snake-spirits'[1] together again in one room!" laughed the twenty-two-year-old daughter of one of them." Her father, the ship captain, had been to dozens of countries, and in the wake of the Cultural Revolution had been jailed for being ideologically tainted by the outside world.

After reading *Hunger Trilogy*, perhaps it will be difficult for the reader to imagine that many of the intellectuals portrayed in part 3, including the author himself, could have the capacity to recall those bleak times—as did the three around the table—with the patience and good humor of parents excusing the past excesses of their children. Intellectuals in the West are captivated and deeply puzzled by the ease with which victims of the Cultural Revolution are seemingly able to forgive the past and look to the future. The reasons for this are extremely complex, providing an endless source of fascination for both foreign intellectual historians of China and thoughtful Chinese themselves. Any answers must surely draw upon ancient Chinese history, philosophy, and perhaps modern psychological analyses of the Chinese mind.[2] This is a problem too large to tackle here, but a look at *Hunger Trilogy*'s depiction of the evolution of twentieth-century Chinese history, the Chinese Communist Party (CCP), and the evolution of the author himself—helps illuminate the problematic subject of Chinese intellectuals and their relationship with the nation and state in this century. What has happened since *Hunger Trilogy* was written in 1979 may also help to explain the willingness of many Chinese intellectuals to look ahead rather than to dwell on the past.

Context

Wang Ruowang wrote *Hunger Trilogy* in 1979 at the height of the "literature of the wounded" (*shanghen wenxue*), which rocked the Chinese literary world with its harsh realistic portrayal of human suffering brought on by the Cultural Revolution.[3] Much of this literature was melodramatic, sentimental, and poorly written, but the key point at the time was that the party allowed it to be published at all (although its appearance certainly aided the cause of the post-Mao leadership).[4] The year *Hunger Trilogy* was written also marked the emergence of a new "literature that delves into life" (*ganyu shenghuo de wenxue*), which adopted as its theme criticism of current political and social problems, thus moving away from a sole concern with exposing the atrocities of the Cultural Revolution. For its time, *Hunger Trilogy* differed from "literature of the wounded" because of a combination of factors: the relatively dispassionate tone of its author (this, despite the autobiographical aspect of the novella); its portrayal of the CCP before 1949 to set it off from the CCP of the Cultural Revolution; its central concern with hunger as a device illustrating the human potential for barbarity; and the fact that, like Liu Binyan's *Renyao zhijian* (People or monsters?),[5] the story itself is true, though strictly speaking it is not reportage.[6] Most important, from the Chinese leadership's point of view, *Hunger Trilogy* went well beyond other "literature of the wounded'' by tackling a previously taboo subject, a firsthand comparison of prison life under the KMT (Guomindang), on the one hand, and the CCP, on the other.

Parallels with Chinese "Towering Wall Literature"

Rather than examine *Hunger Trilogy* in the context of "literature of the wounded," which it went well beyond in many ways,[7] it is more useful to note its affinities with a relatively new genre of literature in contemporary China, which by the mid- to late 1980s was being increasingly referred to as "towering wall literature" (*daqiang wenxue*).

The term "towering wall literature," as currently used in China, refers specifically to the body of post-Mao fiction depicting the life of political prisoners in labor camps from the 1957–58 antirightist campaign to the Cultural Revolution. It should not be confused with "legal literature" (*fazhi wenxue*), which as illustrated in the now defunct Shanghai magazine *Daqiang neiwai* (Inside and outside the towering wall), concerns itself with the present-day lives of petty criminals (as opposed to political prisoners) and cautionary tales about the hardships of prison life, the temptation of criminal activity, and the inevitability of capture for prisoners foolish enough to try escaping.[8]

Towering wall literature, as interpreted by one Chinese scholar in 1988 and apparently accepted by several others, is mainly exemplified by two writers—Cong Weixi, considered the father of this genre, and Zhang Xianliang, its "younger uncle."[9] In 1988 only about ten works of fiction by these two authors were considered part of the prison literature "canon" (the term is mine), making one question if such a small number of pieces actually constitute a bona fide school of literature. It seems natural that writers who had spent time in labor camps or prisons would write about their experiences over the course of the 1980s, as the literary censors loosened up and subjects that had been taboo for decades saw the light of day. But it is unclear to what extent one can label the publication of different writers' accounts of their incarceration a particular kind of literature or even a "trend." The notion of a school of prison literature is weakened by the fact that the scattering of works on this topic that did appear reflect a divergence of literary style and, more important, literary motivation.

For example, in *Nanren de yiban shi nüren* (Half of man is woman), Zhang Xianliang uses the labor camp backdrop more as a foil for the protagonist's almost romantic self-reflection than as the primary focus of dramatic conflict, as is the case in Wang Ruowang's *Hunger Trilogy*.[10] Not unlike other experimental writers of the 1980s in China, Zhang Xianliang explores the psychological and sexual impact of incarceration on the imprisoned individual, focusing just as much on the figurative sense of imprisonment as on its literal reality.[11] But Wang Ruowang, as is typical of his generation (Liu Binyan is probably similar in this respect), concerns himself with an extroverted, straightforward chronicle of a collective experience rather than an internal, more indulgent analysis of an individual battle with evil and lack of freedom.

Perhaps Chinese scholars do not consider *Hunger Trilogy* to fall under the rubric of prison literature because some of the prison life it portrays predates 1949. It is more likely, however, that Wang Ruowang may not be considered a writer of towering wall literature because, unlike Cong Weixi and Zhang Xianliang, he only wrote one work about his prison experiences. It is important to stress, however, that Wang wrote *Hunger Trilogy* at a very early date, 1979, when few writers dared to tackle the sensitive issue of treatment of prisoners under the CCP, let alone a vivid comparison of how the KMT and CCP handled their political prisoners. Cong Weixi's "Daqiang xia de hong yulan" (The blood-stained magnolia), which was completed nine months earlier than *Hunger Trilogy*, also takes place in a prison, but it differs from Wang Ruowang's novella in several respects.

First, unlike *Hunger Trilogy*, Cong Weixi's novel conforms more to "literature of the wounded" than prison literature because of its overly melodramatic tone and melodramatic story line. Second, although the backdrop of "The Blood-Stained Magnolia" is a prison and labor camp, the story is limited in time to 1976 and the power struggle ensuing from the death of Zhou Enlai and the renewed attack against Deng Xiaoping. Third, Cong's novel is not openly autobiographical, while Wang's is, making the latter more bold. Fourth, Cong's dramatic tension lies in the black-and-white struggle of good against evil as manifested in individual characters, whereas Wang uses hunger as the central, unifying tension.[12]

Western Prison Literature

Where does *Hunger Trilogy* fit in with Western novels about hunger and prison life? Nineteenth-century French Romantic writers often viewed the notion of imprisonment as the "tragic beauty of solitude, glorification of the individual and concern for the problem of identity, existential anguish." They saw "salvation through enclosure, insight into darkness—the paradox is rooted in the age-old symbol of the captive soul, in the religious notion of a happy captivity."[13] The Norwegian writer Knut Hamsun's novel *Hunger* (1890) presents an intellectual who follows the voice of his unconscious for ten years, starving himself by living off odd jobs and the meager earnings from his occasional writing. Hamsun's protagonist feels that his suffering "is the right thing; it is the road of genius and of learning. His painful starvation has called up an immense reserve of healing power that had been lying concealed in the psyche."[14]

While Wang Ruowang no doubt makes use of his imprisonment to look inward—indeed, the entire Cultural Revolution experience could not help but have this effect on Chinese intellectuals—*Hunger Trilogy* is steeped in a Chinese rather than Western tradition, and it does not dwell on the individual ego of the narrator or other characters. Similarly, it refrains from glorifying the prison experience in the European Romantic sense. Nor are Wang and his fellow inmates "hungry" in the existential sense of Hamsun's main character. Instead, like many twentieth-century Russian literary treatments of prison life, *Hunger Trilogy* is a chronicle very much rooted in historical time and place, a story and a situation intimately bound to the history of a nation rather then to any one individual. This is not surprising, since Chinese literature does not share the West's focus on the inner workings of the individual as separate from society, nation, and history.

Chinese critics have compared *Hunger Trilogy* to Aleksandr Solzhenitsyn's *The Gulag Archipelago*.[15] Admittedly, it does not approach that work in scope, historical detail, or bibliographic documentation. But there is a more important way in which *Hunger Trilogy* does not compare to an exposé of Stalin's labor camps, and that is in tone. For it is not the author's intention to unmask an inhumane regime. Rather, *Hunger Trilogy* is an attempt to show the evolution of a Chinese national ideal (read political party) in which the author has always believed, and to share the very personal transformation of Chinese intellectuals in their relationship to that ideal. Thus, the reader can see in *Hunger Trilogy* the parallel maturation of a young, bold, idealistic CCP fighting its way against the KMT (part 1), the Japanese (part 2), and, at last, its own internal enemies (part 3), and that of a young, bold, idealistic intellectual such as Wang Ruowang (although he clearly does not limit his portrayal of intellectual "types" to himself) fighting his way *with* the party and the ideals it represents against the same enemies. Thus, unlike authors of prison literature from the Soviet Union and Eastern Europe, Wang Ruowang's "education," as it were, takes place at the same time as the "education" of the Chinese Communist Party. Like the party, the writer is emboldened by early victories against external enemies and then stopped short in his tracks by the most challenging enemy he has ever faced—the enemy within the party. For it was war within the ranks during the Cultural Revolution that left both the CCP and Chinese intellectuals the most vulnerable they had ever been since their relationship began in the 1920s.

Food in Chinese Culture

One cannot fully appreciate the special implications of hunger in China without an awareness of the overriding importance of food in Chinese culture. As far back as the Zhou dynasty (twelfth century to third century B.C.), there are textual references to a cooking vessel as "the prime symbol of the state."[16] Rituals involving food were enormously important, and "the welfare of the entire civilization was evidently thought to depend on the sacrifices and other rituals being performed correctly, which meant above all the right arrangement of vessels and food."[17] In his anthropological study of food in Chinese history, K. C. Chang describes the creative way in which the Chinese, however rich or poor, have made such thorough use of everything available to them for eating, concluding that "food and eating are among things central to the Chinese way of life and part of the Chinese ethos."[18] The elevation of food to a nearly divine status and its pivotal role in society were not limited to ancient Chinese civilization, but "none took it farther than did China."[19]

As one scholar has noted, the Chinese are united by their obsession with good food and cooking. "People discuss food for hours, and almost everyone from the richest to the poorest, from scholar to laborer, from northerner to southerner, is concerned with the best and can tell the observer how to find it."[20] Thus, it is not surprising to find the inmates in part 3 of *Hunger Trilogy* engaged in a distracting but masochistic exercise of recalling the name and specialty of every food stall in the old City God Temple quarter of Shanghai, for "Old Shanghainese could tick them off in order starting from the temple gate entrance without missing a one—like counting the family's jewels" (p. 74).

Indeed, the Chinese language itself reflects this central concern for food. There are endless examples. A few include the traditional daily greeting "Have you eaten yet?" (*Ni chiguo fan meiyou?*), the reference to a lifetime job as an "iron ricebowl" (*tie fanwan*), the term for "population" being literally "human mouth" (*renkou*).[21]

Eating and cooking in China have always been considered great arts. Gourmets have been noted throughout history.[22] The contemporary writer Lu Wenfu has devoted a short story to the subject of a Chinese gourmet and his transformation before and after Liberation from a master of the art of eating to one who, because of this refined ability, is qualified to teach others the theory of fine cooking. An essential point in the story is that the narrator, who transforms a famous restaurant from its pre-1949 "bourgeois" orientation for fine food and service into a bare-bones mediocre restaurant geared toward the post-1949 "masses," is chastised by the very workers whom he assumes his reforms will benefit. The implication is that even the Chinese proletariat is capable of discerning good food from bad and shares the same desire as the wealthier classes for good cooking. Wang Ruowang himself has a strong personal interest in the theory of cooking, having lectured and written about the art.[23]

Another cultural aspect to the preparation and eating of food in China is the degree to which traditional Chinese view cooking and eating as a gentleman's art and a cultural ritual. From this arises the extreme discomfort many Chinese have with the depiction in literature of human beings reduced by starvation to animalistic or childish behavior. Many older Chinese critics reacted negatively to *Hunger Trilogy*'s naturalistic portrayal of such behavior.[24] Even the young narrator in the contemporary short story "Qiwang" (The chess master) is uneasy watching the character Wang Yisheng, deprived of food for some time, devour individual grains of rice in a most ungentlemanly manner.[25]

Hunger Trilogy shows us that hunger, like death, is the great leveler, that no matter what a person's class background or level of intelligence might be, when faced with hunger he or she behaves much the same as anyone else under such circumstances. This notion, which was surely forced upon victims of the Cultural Revolution, is not one that sits well with many Chinese. What greater irony is there than a nation obsessed with food for thousands of years intentionally starving its own people? This image, like the one presented by the writer Lu Xun in "A

Madman's Diary'' (i.e., of men "eating" other men),[26] is projected in the metaphorical as well as the literal sense. If thus intended, one could easily imagine the author employing "hunger" and the primitive behavior it causes to indict the Cultural Revolution, which turned a civilized nation into a barbaric one.

Finally, there is the connection in *Hunger Trilogy* and other Chinese fiction between food and freedom. When prisoner Liu Zhihou in part 3 of *Hunger Trilogy* is unexpectedly released for one day, he spends it eating his way from one restaurant to another, savoring each item seemingly more than freedom itself. In Zhang Xianliang's "Lühuashu" (Mimosa), the narrator is ecstatic at being allowed in the kitchen of the village housing him after his stint in a labor camp, for "only free men could go into the kitchen."[27]

The Writer

Before the plot of *Hunger Trilogy* and the specific ways in which the work illuminates the relationship between the CCP and Chinese intellectuals over time are described, it is necessary to know something about its author and the extent to which his life parallels the events of the novella.[28]

Wang Ruowang's youth conforms with part 1 of *Hunger Trilogy*, which chronicles his three years in a KMT prison in Shanghai, during which time the inmates staged a hunger strike. In 1933 Wang was sixteen years old. He had joined the Communist Party Youth League the previous year, after being expelled from school for his involvement in a student movement, and was working for the CCP underground in a pharmaceutical factory in Shanghai. There he founded "toilet literature" (*cesuo wenxue*), a wall newspaper posted in the workers' latrines where it was safe from the eyes of managers, who used separate toilet facilities. Wang was arrested in May 1934 and sentenced to ten years in prison for his CCP activities, but he was released after three years because of an amnesty proclaimed by Chiang Kai-shek during the Second United Front. Most of the activists with whom he was incarcerated are no longer living, although in 1988 two of them were still alive, one a former governor of Guangdong, the other a former deputy governor of Anhui.[29]

After his release from prison, Wang followed his fellow idealists to the Communists' wartime center of Yan'an. In October 1937 he entered the party at the age of nineteen. Following the same rebellious strains that compelled him to join the CCP in its fight against the KMT and the Japanese, Wang got involved in a controversial wall newspaper at Yan'an called *Qingqidui* (Light cavalry), which party leaders soon criticized for its exposés of the dark side of party life in Yan'an. In 1942 Mao's right-hand man, Kang Sheng, sent Wang in disgrace to Shandong, where he survived ''through the kindness of peasants'' as a kind of barefoot doctor (before the term existed).[30] Shandong is the backdrop for part 2 of *Hunger Trilogy*, which, according to the author, like part 1 is written ''true to life and without exaggeration.''[31] This section of the trilogy recounts the author's flight from Japanese troops in a particularly bleak stretch of rural Shandong, where he and his comrades get lost and are faced with starvation.

After World War II, Wang was pardoned by Kang Sheng and worked in the East China Bureau Propaganda Department and subsequently as co-editor of *Wenyi yuebao*, the precursor of *Shanghai wenxue*. In 1957–58 he was branded a ''rightist'' for a collection of some ten *zawen* (critical essays) he published in response to the Hundred Flowers call, essays that criticized party dogmatism and excessive literary control. The titles of some of these essays reflect his train of thought at the time: ''Bubu shefang'' (Creating barriers step by step), ''Yi ban zhige'' (A partition apart), and ''Buduitou'' (Something amiss). He used the words *barriers* and *partitions* to describe the gap between the leaders and led and between nonparty intellectuals and the party. Wang accused the party of being uninformed about what goes on below it, warning that the more one uses political criteria to label people, ''the more the party will alienate itself from the masses.''[32] Wang struck a chord dangerously sensitive to party leaders in 1957, and he became an early victim of the Antirightist Campaign.[33]

Soon after the party removed his "rightist" label in 1962, Wang criticized the leadership once again. His targets this time were Great Leap Forward policies. In a story called "Yi kou daguo de lishi" (History of a cauldron), he revealed the cruel, impractical, and ironic nature of Great Leap policies that forced peasants to melt down useful implements of production for the national cause. This story led to Wang's being singled out for criticism by Shanghai party boss Ke Qingshi. Wang's wife, already on the road to mental collapse due to the government's persecution of her family, died in 1964 as a result of this renewed attack on her husband.[34]

It was no surprise, then, that in 1966 Wang was incarcerated in Shanghai as a "counterrevolutionary." There he found himself in the same prison building he had occupied as a prisoner under the KMT regime in the 1930s. He remained there for four years. All of the characters in part 3 of *Hunger Trilogy*—which graphically and relentlessly depicts daily life during this stint in prison, where food was almost nonexistent—are based on real people. Wang Ruowang did not portray his good friends the ship captain and the businessman, referred to at the opening of this introduction, nor did he describe all of the cellmates still alive today. Instead, he chose to portray individuals who represented certain types and who evinced certain typical responses of one kind or another to hunger and oppression during the Cultural Revolution.

There is one further point worth noting about the degree to which *Hunger Trilogy* reflects real events in Wang's life. In spring 1989 the Chinese press quoted Wang as saying, "I'm not only the founder of bourgeois liberalization, I'm also the founder of the hunger strike because I've gone on hunger strikes four times in my life."[35] If the latter part of this remark is accurate, this minor inconsistency conforms with what we know about *Hunger Trilogy* and its relation to Wang's real life: some concessions to literary convention and drama were made in the work, but the events themselves and most of the people in them are true to life.

Why did Wang Ruowang write *Hunger Trilogy*? "At the

time, I swore to those who had died in prison that if I ever got out of there alive, I would spend the rest of my life struggling with that bunch of inhumane pseudo-Marxists. Since those veteran comrades who died before their time could no longer speak for themselves about their grievances, I would speak for them."[36] "The dead cannot speak but the living can. I have a responsibility to tell the truth as I saw it."[37] Indeed, after his full rehabilitation in 1979, Wang wrote with a vengeance, producing almost as many *zawen* and short stories as he did over the three-decade span between 1933 and 1962.[38] In this way he feverishly delivered himself of the anger he and so many of his generation had borne in silence for twenty years. One month after Wang completed *Hunger Trilogy*, the Fourth National Writers' Conference encouraged a bolder brand of literature, thus fueling his need for catharsis. And despite the major setback delivered in the exhortation for writers to consider the "social effects" (*shehui xiaoguo*) of their work at the February 1980 Drama Conference in Beijing, Wang continued to launch controversial attacks against what he considered the "remnants of ultra-leftist thinking."[39] One of these attacks took the form of a short story written around the time of *Hunger Trilogy*. Called " 'Shangxin gou' daixu" (By way of a preface to "The Sad Canal") and also based on a true story, it is an account of Wang's investigation of a young teacher's indictment of local leaders' bungled handling of an irrigation problem that deeply and deleteriously affected people's lives in a county near Shanghai.[40] As a result of the author's intervention, the young teacher is spared punishment for sending his exposé to a Shanghai literary journal (Wang's). In contrast to *Hunger Trilogy*, this story is more in line with Wang's post-1979 writing that concerned itself with current problems rather than recalling the bad days of the Cultural Revolution, although the writer has always linked present problems to political and social habits adopted during the Cultural Revolution.

Hunger Trilogy

Hunger Trilogy is probably the only openly published post-1949 work of PRC fiction solely devoted to the treatment of hunger in such excruciating detail. It was also, as far as I know, the first openly published post-Mao autobiographical treatment of prison life during the Cultural Revolution. And it is the only novella in China to use hunger as a foil against which three eras of Chinese history—the CCP–KMT united front struggle of the 1930s, the War of Resistance Against Japan of the 1940s, and the Cultural Revolution of the 1960s—are illuminated and contrasted by an intellectual who lived through them all as agitator, victim, and, alas, patient observer.

Although the novella is autobiographical in the sense that it relates true events in the author's life, it is written more in the style of reportage, with the author as recorder of events rather than central participant. Indeed, Wang purposely reveals little about his own personal predicament at this time beyond his own physical and emotional reaction to hunger, which is recounted in the same voice as that describing others' reactions to the same hunger. Indeed, the author never intended for his voice to intrude on the recitation of events, and aside from an outburst of bewilderment and pain in part 3, it rarely does. On the other hand, one could argue that as in literature of this kind, although the writer does not impose his personality on the narration of events, he is in evidence everywhere throughout the work, as an author's own biases and background cannot but influence his choice of subject, presentation, and tone.[41]

The Intellectual, the Nation, and the Party: Growing Up Together

The most distinct thread that runs through *Hunger Trilogy* is the maturation process of the nation, the CCP, and the intellectuals who believe in both. This process is reflected in the lives of the author and several characters, some of whom appear in part 1 and again in part 3. By observing the transformation of their beliefs over a course of several decades, the author has traced the psychological and emotional development not only of individuals, but of the nation as manifested in the values of these individuals. Wang uses the characters of three different people to show three various "types" of responses to Chinese history and events of the last forty years: Xu Yushu, the true believer who dies the wiser and who appears in parts 1 and 3; Old Zhou, the true believer who dies none the wiser and who appears indirectly in part 2 and in person in part 3; and Gu Guanshi, the potential true believer whose faith is entirely shattered by the Cultural Revolution, resulting in his return to the United States. We meet Dr. Gu in part 3. It is likely that Wang Ruowang sees himself and his own values reflected in all three of these characters.

Xu Yushu

We first encounter Xu in part 1 on the first day the sixteen-year-old Wang Ruowang (known then by his real name, Wang Shouhua) is thrown into the KMT prison. Xu is an intellectual who had studied in Japan and subsequently took to tutoring Wang in Japanese. Xu is a reserved man, but a staunch believer in the CCP. ''Some day our Red Army will fight its way to Shanghai. . . . As soon as our Red Army gets here and opens the gates, it'll be like the Bastille gates being thrown open by the flood of the French Revolution in 1789—in one day all the prisoners were freed, even those sentenced to death'' (p. 5). Wang, who cried at his first glimpse of the cell he was to occupy for the next ten years, was moved. ''He spoke with such faith and confidence that I was completely entranced by the beautiful picture he painted. . . . I didn't cry anymore, and recovered my youthful vigor.'' Even when Xu realizes that the Red Army has retreated to Northwest China, he continues to encourage the young boy, who is gradually growing despondent about ever getting out of jail. ''As long as the Red Army hasn't left China, the day to 'open the door' [referring to a term from their Japanese lesson] will come,'' (p. 8) assures the confident Xu. It is Xu Yushu who suggests that the prisoners stage a hunger strike when conditions get unbearable, and, despite his own bout with beriberi, he continues to offer much comfort to the youth, slipping Wang a sesame cake when there is no food left in the cell several days into the strike. The striking prisoners eventually emerge victorious, presumably because their KMT wardens were under pressure not to let Communist political prisoners die in jail during the KMT–CCP United Front.

The next time we see Xu Yushu is in part 3, some thirty years later. He looked, according to Wang, like "a man with one foot in the grave" (p. 117). Wang had accidentally discovered his former Japanese teacher in a solitary confinement cell in the same prison in which Wang was incarcerated in Shanghai. Wang tells us through Xu that Wang Hongwen and others in the radical regime (now known as the "Gang of Four") were attempting to smear the reputations of pre-1949 underground party workers in Shanghai by going through Xu, who refused to cooperate. "Afterward," says Xu, "they used torture. . . . they brought a bunch of thugs who tried four at a time to make me confess. When I wouldn't admit to anything, one of them twisted my head, two grabbed my feet, and they flung me in mid-air, slamming my backbone against the floor. In the old days when the Guomindang caught me, they used torture too. But the torture used by 'our own people' is somewhat more civilized. They beat you quite meticulously so that no scars or bruises show." Xu believes he is close to death and has little time to speak with Wang, who must return to his own cell. He asks Wang to make sure the truth about Xu and his colleagues in the underground is known, and that the lies of the radicals are exposed. Wang tells us, "He stopped for a while, then said, disjointedly, 'Have you ever considered that in the enemy's prison I got beriberi and didn't die? Instead, I'll die in a prison of the proletarian dictatorship. Could fate really toy with people like this?' " (p. 119). Xu Yushu's faith in the CCP is not diminished as a result of his torture, but it has wavered. Xu lives to be released from prison a very sick man. Wang, also freed, visits his mentor in Huashan Hospital, knowing Xu is about to die. "Seeing Xu Yushu this time frightened me. His face had become a bit deformed, the blue veins at his temples were twitching slightly, and his voice had weakened." Xu shares a revelation. "I'll be going to see Marx with a clear conscience . . . except that I'm unable to face the party because in 1957 and 1958 I mistook more than ten high-level intellectuals for rightists, when really they were all talented people working for the nation. . . . We didn't prevent the rise of the 'Gang of Four' earlier because we didn't use our heads; we blindly believed in the 'highest directive' [i.e., Mao Zedong]. This is a disgrace for a Communist Party member. Because of my blindness, I treated my own comrades as enemies. . . . We were punished for this'' (pp. 132–33).

Thus, we see the character of Xu Yushu as the loyal party member who starts out as a confident, activist underground party leader in the 1930s to become a beaten, albeit more enlightened man in the 1970s. For despite Xu's continuing belief in the party and the nation (his dying words give instructions on how to develop China's underground natural resources), he has awakened to the fact that blind faith is actually detrimental to China and the CCP, and that both would be in better shape if true believers such as himself had been wise enough to question mistaken policies.[42] Here Wang shows us how the party shot itself in the foot with its anti-intellectual campaigns, damaging the successful, idealistic foundation it had laid during the 1930s with the faith of high-minded people such as Xu Yushu.

Old Zhou

While Xu Yushu lives to understand the mistakes of the party as well as his own, Old Zhou does not. We first meet him in part 2 indirectly through his then fiancée, Wang Lei. He is "Young Zhou" then, a young revolutionary who has joined the Eighth Route Army in Shandong. Thirty years later, in part 3, he is a member of the Shanghai Municipal Committee who has been targeted by Jiang Qing, Zhang Chunqiao, and Ma Tianshui[43] for persecution because of his reports on their unethical behavior, and winds up in Wang Ruowang's prison cell. Zhou is a true believer who, during their short time together, cautions Wang Ruowang against speaking his mind. "Don't complain," he admonishes Wang. "This revolution was launched by the old man himself!" (p. 104). Then, later, "You old fool! It's not in vogue now to speak the truth. Don't you know that yet? We should uphold and protect the party's prestige wherever we are!" (p. 105).

Wang is baffled by Zhou's unquestioning faith at such a time. "Do you mean to say that we should rely on lies to maintain the party's reputation?" (p. 5) asks the younger Wang. Zhou eventually contracts hepatitis in prison and dies. The author tells us he learned much from him. "He was the first person to make me realize exactly what rubbish the so-called leadership of the proletariat was!" (p. 110).

The portrayal of Old Zhou was a conscious effort on the part of the author to present the dilemma of a type of Chinese revolutionary and intellectual. "He was such a good Communist," writes Wang. "His crime stemmed from his loyalty to the party" (p. 113).[44] After Wang was released from prison, he visited Zhou's widow, the Wang Lei from part 2. Zhou's remains lay in a wooden urn on her dresser. "A veteran party member, strong and full of energy, who had struggled all his life, was reduced overnight to nothing but ash. What more was there to say?" writes Wang (p. 123).

When discussing *Hunger Trilogy*, Wang describes Old Zhou as the kind of person who meekly submits to ill treatment and adversity (*nilai shunshou*). Although the author writes in part 3 that he respects Zhou for being more politically cautious than Wang himself, nine years after writing *Hunger Trilogy*, Wang admitted to having a serious problem accepting the kind of submission Zhou's life embodied.[45] Indeed, the problem of Old Zhou remains a source of heartache and embarrassment for Chinese intellectuals, both for those who responded to the Cultural Revolution in a similar manner and for those, like Wang Ruowang, who did not. The exposure of the willingly submissive element of the Chinese psyche that some perceive as contributing to China's national weakness throughout history was also a theme that tortured Lu Xun, as shown through his character portrayal of Ah Q.[46]

Gu Guanshi

Like Bai Hua's patriotic protagonist in "Kulian" (Bitter love),[47] Gu Guanshi is an intellectual who was trained in the United

States and returns to China in the 1950s despite the alternative of a better life abroad. Dr. Gu, director of the Chest Hospital in Shanghai, is by no means a proponent of Western lifestyles. He had once been imprisoned in the United States for incomplete immigration papers, and like many Chinese there during the McCarthy era, faced much discrimination. It is natural, then, that upon entering the prison in Shanghai he feels more comfortable than in the foreign prison. His crime is "divulging state secrets" by sharing with an old classmate visiting from the United States his discovery of acupuncture as an anesthetic during surgery. Unlike Xu Yushu and Old Zhou, Gu Guanshi is not a party member. Thus, it is somewhat easier for him to question the logic of his treatment by the Cultural Revolution leadership, and to admit the folly of his patriotic feelings toward a country whose present regime does not want him. "Is it possible that the motherland my wife and I sought is this savage and lawless nation? Ah! I was blind, like a moth attracted to a lamp, I threw myself at the light only to destroy my life!" (p. 84). After the real doctor on whom the Gu character is based got out of prison, he and his wife moved to the United States, where Wang Ruowang believes they still reside.

Dr. Gu's bitter reaction to the maltreatment he and his wife endured in the Cultural Revolution underscores the price China has had to pay for the persecution of its talented intellectuals—the ultimate alienation and departure from China of many of them. It is evident from Wang Ruowang's other writings and from lengthy discussions with him that he sees himself in each of the three characters above—Xu Yushu, Old Zhou, and Gu Guanshi. Like Xu Yushu, Wang has always viewed himself as a loyal party member, but not one without dark spots in his past. For Wang, too, has admitted to errors in his treatment of others, errors based on a willingness to follow the political winds of the time.[48] Like Old Zhou, Wang genuinely shares a respect for the CCP's accomplishments and for what the party has historically represented. Where he differs from Zhou is in his ability to question openly the direction the party took in the 1960s and 1970s, although had Zhou lived, perhaps he would have ended up with similar doubts. As for Gu Guanshi, Wang shares his patriotism and need to examine the ironic rewards and punishments of national loyalty.

The Author's Loss of Innocence

Wang's own maturity, evolving values, and relationship with the party can be traced from the beginning of part 1 to the end of part 3 of *Hunger Trilogy*. He enters the KMT jail in part 1 as a crying sixteen-year-old boy, the youngest in his cell. The heady success of the hunger strike and the courageous words and actions of his revolutionary cellmates leave him more determined than ever to join the CCP, which he does at Yan'an in 1937 after his release from prison. By part 3, thirty years later, everything has changed. Rather than being the youngest in his cell, at forty-eight years old he is the oldest. Perhaps the biggest difference is illustrated by the reasons he imagines a hunger strike to demand more and better food would not work now as it had in the KMT jail. A hunger strike, he feels, would be a futile, lethal exercise. For one thing, his fellow inmates are not as unified in philosophy and purpose as his 1934 comrades and would not easily agree to a hunger strike. Moreover, the CCP jailors would like nothing better than for their charges to die of starvation, thereby decreasing the number of "ants" to feed. The prisoners' lack of purpose and cohesion is the key to Wang's wavering of faith in the system in part 3. In the Nationalist prison of the 1930s, physical perseverance was more manageable because everyone knew who the enemy was—the KMT. But in the Shanghai prison of the Cultural Revolution, emotional and intellectual confusion compounded physical hardship because of a lack of understanding of who the enemy really was—one's own party or elements who had usurped one's party?[49] By part 3, Wang questions himself. During efforts to discourage a youth from committing suicide, Wang urges him to believe in the "New China," while to himself he admits, "The fact was, though, that I felt as insecure as he did" (p. 85).

Wang cannot but make comparisons between the KMT jail of the 1930s and that of the CCP in the late 1960s, especially after discovering that the very interrogation room into which he is taken in the 1960s is the same one in which he was once interrogated by his Guomindang enemies. Every detail in the room is the same, with one exception—the portrait of Mao hanging on the far wall. The author cannot help but wonder at the astounding irony of this turn of fate. When Wang emerges from prison with prematurely white hair, he has a question. "The Guomindang reactionaries [in 1934] had sentenced me to ten years, but I was freed after serving only three and a half. I had always rejoiced over my good fortune. Who would have thought that after the revolution succeeded, I'd have to pay off that free time I earned through sheer luck by serving time in a CCP prison? Was this personal destiny or just a tragedy of the times?" (p. 121).

Wang's portrayal of other characters, beyond the three described above, underscores his theme of ardent, idealistic youth turned skeptical and, in some cases, cynical. Wang Lei, shown in part 2 as the fresh, beautiful, naive, and generous fiancée of a revolutionary (then Young Zhou), reappears at the end of part 3 when the author visits her house to console her after her husband's death in prison. "I hardly recognized her. Shocks and tragedies had so crushed this once brave and lively young woman that she now looked like Xiang Lin's wife from the movie. Her eyes were dull and dark. Her once dimpled cheeks were now all wrinkled" (pp. 122–23). Wang Lei's former idealism, marked by extreme naiveté in part 2, has been completely overshadowed by personal suffering and loss, as exemplified in her loss of hair, a result of her own imprisonment and depression.

An equally poignant character used to illustrate the loss of innocence and faith of both the author and the country as a whole is the young school teacher whose suicide Wang witnesses in the middle of the night in their Shanghai cell. No attempts on the part of the older men in the cell to give him incentives to go on living are effective. Ashamed that he had implicated his fiancée under torture, he attempts suicide twice, meeting his objective the second time. His fellow inmates had learned little about him, but his senseless death leaves a deep mark on all of them as a symbol of the irrational decay around them.

The Reward of Experience

Lest readers get the impression that the author intended *Hunger Trilogy* to paint an entirely bleak picture of the CCP and contemporary China, it is important to point out that like the character Xu Yushu, the author genuinely believes that he "may die without regrets" about the dark episodes described here. For returning to the three former "cow-devils and snake-spirits" sitting around the table in Shanghai on a spring afternoon in 1988, they and many others like them who lived through the events of part 3 agree that China needed a Cultural Revolution in order to wake up from its complacency about itself as a nation and its place in the world. Although it would be easy to dismiss such feelings as a defense mechanism for warding off the horrors of the past, many Chinese intellectuals are able to place their personal experiences in the broader context of thousands of years of Chinese history and view their personal sacrifices as ultimately beneficial to the nation. As one of the former inmates remarked that day in 1988, raising his thumb and forefinger to form a small space, "What is a sacrifice of ten years in the centuries-long history of China?" On the lighter side, it was pointed out to this foreigner that none of these three would ever have been friends if it weren't for the fact of their sharing adversity twenty years ago, for in China a businessman, a ship captain, and a writer would otherwise have no basis for a friendship like theirs.

This ability to learn from history, certainly a tradition in China, has been reflected in the political, social, and economic policies implemented in the PRC since the late 1970s by the post-Mao leadership.[50] Because of the economic and social liberalization promoted by Chinese leaders in the 1980s, and because of a more liberal literary policy that permitted realistic portrayals of present-day life, Chinese writers in the 1980s turned their attention away from the Cultural Revolution and the mistakes of the past. Even Wang Ruowang, a fierce proponent of remembering the past, focused most of his writing on the present.[51] One exception is his autobiography *Ziwo ganjue lianghao* (Feeling good), which discusses the past, but in an intentionally uncontroversial manner.[52] Wang worked on his autobiography at home during periods of retreat, when it was necessary for political reasons to lie low. The anti–bourgeois liberalization campaigns of 1981 and 1987 were such times. During the 1981 campaign, he was advised to retire from his editorial post at *Shanghai Literature*. There were other, less publicized stretches of time between 1981 and 1987 when he was forced for similar reasons to write quietly at home.

Perhaps indicative of Wang's own confidence in the positive changes that took place between the writing of *Hunger Trilogy* in 1979 and the student democracy movement of 1989 is the degree to which during that decade he felt free to write about social, economic, and political problems that arose from the looser economic policies of the 1980s. Indeed, Wang was perceived to have overstepped the acceptable boundaries imposed on him as a CCP member when he was expelled from the CCP in January 1987 for his alleged role in encouraging the student movement at the end of the previous year.[53] Yet despite his loss of party membership, until June 1989 Wang was free to write as he wished at home and to maintain the same personal and many of the same professional contacts he had always enjoyed. That freedom ended in September 1989.

Wang Ruowang was a vocal supporter of the student demonstrations of spring 1989. On June 14, 1989, he went into hiding in the countryside, returning to Shanghai on July 19 at the urging of friends who did not expect his arrest. Once back home he was placed under house arrest, and then formally arrested on September 8, three months after the tragic events of early June, now known as the Tiananmen Square Massacre. Following the usual pattern of political crackdowns against intellectuals (with which

Wang is intimately familiar), the CCP denounced him in several lengthy articles in the Chinese press. He was accused, in the main, of "listening to the Voice of America and spreading rumors based on its broadcasts, writing articles in support of the student hunger strike, giving counterrevolutionary speeches on Shanghai's People's Square, and publishing articles in the Hong Kong press." He was further accused of trying to "overthrow the party's leadership" through his writing.[54] While many of the other older leading advocates of the student movement have avoided arrest by leaving China, Wang did not, and the authorities have chosen an easy target. Due to his bent for vocal dissent and his colorful personality, Wang Ruowang has served as a convenient scapegoat in party purges dating back almost fifty years.

Wang Ruowang's incarceration in a Shanghai prison from September 8, 1989, to October 29, 1990, during which time he was allowed no contact with his family, marked the writer's third imprisonment (following the two documented in this volume). Although now free to live at home with his wife, he must report regularly to the authorities, is not permitted to leave Shanghai without approval, and will probably find it impossible to travel abroad, despite longstanding invitations to do so. It seems at the time of writing that the CCP has not yet learned its lesson from history, as have the seventy-three-year-old author and some of the other characters in *Hunger Trilogy*, but it is inevitable that the party will be forced to do so before long.

Notes

1. "Cow-devils and snake-spirits" is a phrase from Chinese mythology used during the Cultural Revolution to refer to anyone who was the focus of attack during that era—intellectuals, "capitalists," and the like.

2. See Arthur Kleinman, *Social Origins of Distress and Disease: Depression, Neurasthenia, and Pain in Modern China* (New Haven: Yale University Press, 1986). This is based on the author's work at Hunan Medical College examining post–Cultural Revolution mental patients. Anne F. Thurston's "Victims of China's Cultural Revolution: The Invisible Wounds," part 1, *Pacific Affairs* 57, 4 (Winter 1984–85): 599–620, and part 2, 58, 1 (Spring 1985): 5–27, is based on interviews with Cultural Revolution victims. She

concludes that Chinese patriotism is a central factor affecting victims' ability to cope and to focus on the future (part 2, pp. 26–27). An enlightening first-hand account of survival by an intellectual during the Cultural Revolution and other movements is found in Yue Daiyun and Carolyn Wakeman, *To the Storm: The Odyssey of a Revolutionary Chinese Woman* (Berkeley: University of California Press, 1985). See also Merle Goldman with Timothy Cheek and Carol Lee Hamrin, eds., *China's Intellectuals and the State: In Search of a New Relationship* (Cambridge: Harvard University Press, 1987), especially pp. 1–20. For a discussion of the intellectual tradition in China, see Jerome B. Grieder, *Intellectuals and the State in Modern China: A Narrative History* (New York: The Free Press, 1981).

3. This is also referred to as "scar literature." See Perry Link, ed., *Stubborn Weeds: Popular and Controversial Chinese Literature after the Cultural Revolution* (Bloomington: Indiana University Press, 1983), p. 20; and Perry Link, ed., *Roses and Thorns: The Second Blooming of the Hundred Flowers in Chinese Fiction 1979–80* (Berkeley: University of California Press, 1984), p. 20. Link's introductions to both these anthologies provide a succinct history of the literature of this period. See also Kyna Rubin, "An Interview with Mr. Wang Ruowang," *China Quarterly* (September 1981): 501–3.

4. Link, *Roses and Thorns*, p. 20.

5. "People or Monsters?" in *People or Monsters? and Other Stories and Reportage from China after Mao*, ed. Perry Link (Bloomington: Indiana University Press, 1983), pp. 11–68. The original Chinese is in *Renmin wenxue*, 1979, no. 9.

6. "Reportage (*baogao wenxue*) is a modern Chinese genre that falls between literary art and news report. Good reportage differs from ordinary news reporting in several ways: it is longer and more carefully written, and while it may begin from an event in the news, its author seeks to uncover aspects of the social background that are more basic and enduring than the news event itself." Link, *People or Monsters?*, p. 11. For a lengthy investigation of the origins of *texie* and *baogao wenxue*, see Rudolph G. Wagner's "Liu Binyan and the *Texie*," *Modern Chinese Literature* 2, 1 (Spring 1986): 63–98.

7. Li Qing, *Teding shiqi de daqiang wenxue* (Shenyang: Liaoning daxue chubanshe), 1988, pp. 16–19.

8. See, for example, Wang Fei, ed., *Daqiang neiwai*, 1989, 10 (no. 14) (Shanghai: Daqiang neiwai zazhi she). For a further discussion of *fazhi wenxue*, see Li Qing, *Teding shiqi de daqiang wenxue*, pp. 20–21.

I wish to thank Jeffrey Kinkley and Philip Williams for their thoughts concerning 1980s' "prison literature." Prof. Kinkley discovered "prison literature" during his 1989 trip to China to investigate contemporary Chinese crime fiction. Prof. Williams is conducting a study of *daqiang wenxue*.

9. Li Qing, *Teding shiqi de daqiang wenxue*, pp. 20–21ff. Philip Williams includes Lao Gui (the pen name of Ma Bo) as having written in the mode of "towering wall literature."

10. *Nanren de yiban shi nüren*, by Zhang Xianliang, originally appeared in *Shouhuo*, 1985, no. 5: 4–102, and was reprinted in *Zhang Xianliang ji*

(Fuzhou: Haixia wenyi chuban she, 1986), pp. 385–592.

11. Zhao Zhenkai's "Xingfu dajie shisan hao" (No. 13 Happiness Street) is a notable example of the fictional treatment of imprisonment used in the figurative or expressionistic sense, as argued in Philip Williams's paper, "Zhao Zhenkai's 'Number Thirteen Happiness Street,' " *Journal of the Chinese Language Teachers Association* 25, 1 (1990). The story by Zhao Zhenkai (also known as Bei Dao) is in *Bodong* (Hong Kong: Chinese University Press of Hong Kong, 1985), pp. 201–16. An English translation appears in Geremie Barmé and John Minford, eds., *Seeds of Fire: Chinese Voices of Conscience* (Hong Kong: Far Eastern Economic Review, 1986), pp. 2–16; another English translation is in Bei Dao's *Waves*, ed. Bonnie S. McDougall (New York: New Directions, 1990).

12. *Daqiang xia de hong yulan* originally appeared in *Shouhuo*, 1979, no. 2. It was reprinted in Cong Weixi's *Cong Weixi ji* (Fuzhou: Haixia wenyi chubanshe, 1986), pp. 1–68. It was translated into English in *Chinese Literature* (April 1980): 3–56.

13. Victor Brombert, *The Romantic Prison: The French Tradition* (Princeton: Princeton University Press, 1978), pp. 9 and 17, respectively.

14. Knut Hamsun, *Hunger*, trans. Robert Bly (New York: Farrar, Straus and Giroux, 1967), p. xxii.

15. Aleksandr I. Solzhenitsyn, *The Gulag Archipelago 1918–1956: An Experiment in Literary Investigation*, part 1 (New York: Harper and Row, 1973, 1974); part 2 (1978). According to Wang Ruowang (May 1988 talks with the author), there were no published criticisms of *Hunger Trilogy*. Thus I rely on word of mouth for accounts of critics' reactions to the novella (see note 24 below).

16. K. C. Chang, ed., *Food in Chinese Culture: Anthropological and Historical Perspectives* (New Haven: Yale University Press, 1977), p. 11.

17. E. N. Anderson, *The Food of China* (New Haven: Yale University Press, 1988), p. 21.

18. Chang, *Food in Chinese Culture*, pp. 13–14.

19. Anderson, *The Food of China*, p. 204.

20. Ibid., p. 112.

21. Sun Longji has explored "Chinese orality" in a book published in Hong Kong. For an English translation of excerpts, see Barmé and Minford, eds., *Seeds of Fire*.

22. Chang, *Food in Chinese Culture*, p. 13.

23. Lu Wenfu, "Meishijia" (The gourmet), *Chinese Literature* (Winter 1985): 50–111. Wang Ruowang has published an article on cooking, "Zhongguo pengren chutan" (A preliminary exploration of Chinese cooking), *Zhongguo pengren*, 1986, 11 (no. 63): 4–6. He also once lectured on cooking to an army audience in Jinhua, Zhejiang, in 1985.

24. I thank Professor Huang Ziping of Peking University for sharing with me his valuable thoughts on Chinese critics' reactions to *Hunger Trilogy* and his ideas on the theme of hunger in Chinese literature more generally (correspondence with Prof. Huang, June 1988).

25. Ah Cheng, "The Chess Master," *Chinese Literature* (Summer 1985).

The original Chinese is in *Shanghai wenxue*, 1984, no. 7; another English translation appears in Ah Cheng's *Three Kings: Three Stories from Today's China*, trans. Bonnie S. McDougall (London: Collins Harvill, 1990).

26. Lu Xun, "A Madman's Diary," in *Selected Works of Lu Hsun, Volume One* (Beijing: Foreign Languages Press, 1956), pp. 8–21.

27. Zhang Xianliang, "Mimosa," *Chinese Literature* (Spring 1985), p. 18. The original Chinese (*Lühuashu*) appeared in *Shiyue* in 1984.

28. Wang was born in 1918 in Wujin County, Jiangsu Province. For a more complete outline of his life, see Kyna Rubin, "Keeper of the Flame: Wang Ruowang as Moral Critic of the State," in *China's Intellectuals and the State*, ed. Goldman, pp. 234–50; and Rubin, "An Interview with Mr. Wang Ruowang."

29. Talks with Wang Ruowang, May 1988.

30. Rubin, "An Interview with Mr. Wang Ruowang," pp. 509–10.

31. Talks with Wang Ruowang, May 1988.

32. This quotation is from "Shi 'luohou fenzi,' " *Wenhui bao*, May 27, 1957. "Creating Barriers Step by Step," *Wenhui bao*, April 26, 1957; "A Partition Apart," *Xinwen ribao*, May 7, 1957; the author never intended "Something Amiss" for publication. See Rubin, "An Interview with Mr. Wang Ruowang," pp. 506–7.

33. For an explanation of the Antirightist Campaign against writers and the criticism of Wang Ruowang and his work, see Hualing Nieh, ed., *Literature of the Hundred Flowers*, vol. 1: *Criticism and Polemics*, pp. 237–58, and vol. 2: *Poetry and Fiction*, pp. 372–88 (New York: Columbia University Press, 1981).

34. Rubin, "An Interview with Mr. Wang Ruowang," p. 507. "History of a Cauldron" appeared in *Shanghai wenxue* (July 1962).

35. *Renmin ribao* (overseas edition), September 27, 1989, p. 5.

36. "Wang Ruowang tan wenyi zhengce ji gaige," interview with Guan Yuqian, *Jiushi niandai* (The nineties), 1986, 8: 81.

37. Rubin, "An Interview with Mr. Wang Ruowang," p. 506.

38. Rubin, "Keeper of the Flame," p. 241.

39. See ibid. for examples of Wang's controversial writing of the early 1980s.

40. "By Way of a Preface to 'The Sad Canal,' " translated by Kyna Rubin in *Perspectives in Contemporary Chinese Literature*, ed. Mason Y. H. Wang (University Center, MI: Green River Press, 1983), pp. 137–68. The original Chinese appeared in *Shanghai wenxue*, 1980, no. 6: 36–43, 52.

41. Rudolph G. Wagner, in "The Chinese Writer in His Own Mirror: Writer, State, and Society—the Literary Evidence," has written a fascinating analysis of Chinese writers' relationship with their subject. See Goldman et al., eds., *China's Intellectuals and the State*, pp. 183–231.

42. Liu Binyan's controversial "Di er zhong zhongcheng" (Second kind of loyalty), *Kaituo*, 1985, no. 1: 4–53, is devoted to the theme of dishonest loyalty (to the CCP) rewarded and pure, unquestioning loyalty punished.

43. Ma Tianshui was associated with the Shanghai Municipal Revolutionary Committee since its inception in 1967, serving as one of its vice-chairmen

and as a secretary of the Shanghai Municipal CCP. In 1976 he came under fire as one of the leading members of the "Jiang Qing counterrevolutionary clique in Shanghai."

44. Again, Liu Binyan's "Second Kind of Loyalty" comes to mind here.

45. Talks with Wang Ruowang, May 1988.

46. Lu Xun, "The True Story of Ah Q," *Selected Works of Lu Hsun, Volume One* (Beijing: Foreign Languages Press, 1956), pp. 76–135.

47. *Kulian* appeared in *Shiyue*, 1979, no. 3. For a discussion of the Bai Hua affair, see Leo Ou-fan Lee, "Literary Policy in the People's Republic of China: A Position Paper," in *Mainland China, Taiwan, and U.S. Policy* (Cambridge: Oelgeschlager, Gunn, and Hain, 1983), pp. 103–14.

48. Rubin, "An Interview with Mr. Wang Ruowang," p. 510.

49. Thurston shares the same observation in "Victims of China's Cultural Revolution," part 1, p. 613.

50. For a detailed discussion of political policies since 1978 and their effect on intellectuals, see Carol Lee Hamrin's "Conclusion: New Trends under Deng Xiaoping and his Successors" in *China's Intellectuals and the State*, ed. Goldman et al., pp. 275–304. Hamrin concludes that the new policies and national goals hold promise for intellectuals, and she maintains that long-term view despite the events of June 4, 1989, which she sees as a temporary setback to progressive changes in China that are inevitable and will ultimately benefit intellectuals, even though these changes may not be won without violence. "The Impact of the 1989 Crisis on Intellectuals in China," talk by Carol Hamrin, February 28, 1990, SAIS China Forum, Washington, D.C.

51. Wang's writing, particularly in the mid- and late 1980s, dealt with topics on current economic reform, family, love, theater, traveling, cooking, Chinese customs, and a variety of topics related to present-day life.

52. Parts of the autobiography have already been published. See "Xiaoxiao shinian" (A mere ten years), *Haixia*, 1982, no. 6; "Dierci jiehun," *Qingnian yidai*, 1985, no. 1. At the time of this writing, the next installment, entitled "Shenyi" (Spirit doctor), scheduled for publication in *Huacheng* in 1987, has not yet been released.

53. A plethora of articles criticizing Wang appeared in the press from January through spring 1987. See, for example, *Renmin ribao* (overseas edition), January 20, 1987, p. 2 (trans. in JPRS-CAR-87-011, June 25, 1987, pp. 4–8); *Zhongguo qingnian bao*, January 15, 1987, p. 1 (trans. in JPRS-CPS-87-019, April 7, 1987, pp. 27–41); and *China Daily*, January 15, 1987, p. 1.

54. *Wenhuibao*, October 20, 1989, p. 3; *Jiefang ribao*, October 20, 1989; *Wenxuebao*, December 14, 1989; *Renmin ribao*, January 6, 1990, p. 2 (an abridgement of the preceding article); *Renmin ribao* (overseas edition), September 27, 1989, p. 5.

Hunger Trilogy

Part 1

I DON'T know who it was that invented the religious-like ceremony called "eating a meal to recall bitterness." They say it's conducted to teach you not to forget class bitterness. On a certain day, at the same time, members of entire organizations or military companies eat steamed rolls made of chaff and carrot leaves. If no carrot leaves are available, sweet potato seedlings are used. Everyone has to eat one or two, even people with ulcers. They say eating a few of these rolls gives you a proletarian consciousness and prevents you from becoming revisionist. You're not allowed to knit your brow when you eat, you have to look like you're consciously accepting reform. But if you really have to make a face it's okay, because you can make it part of the game by saying, "I'm thinking about the suffering of the past and the happiness of the present. It makes me sad to think how I was oppressed under the old society."

As for me, when I swallow these rolls I have quite a different reaction. My past suffering was not from eating coarse food, but from the inability to scrounge up even anything coarse to eat, for I've encountered extraordinary hunger, the kind of hunger that makes you wish for death.

And now I want to describe to you the three times I experienced this sort of hunger. I'm not telling you this to strengthen any sort of proletarian consciousness, but to express a hope. Twice is bad enough, three times is too much; I only hope not to have to face starvation a fourth time.

I

A youth of just sixteen was dragged like a criminal into an interrogation room. They made him sit on a big, hard chair. Leather straps on both arms bound him, lest he try to harm the judge.

Accompanied by a clerk, the judge sat on the bench. Looking down from his lofty position, he read the court "verdict":

> Punishing severely in accordance with the laws against threatening social order during a time of emergency, but taking into account the young age of the offender, this court sentences the offender to ten years imprisonment, sentence to begin this year of 1934, in the month of . . . , day of . . .

To sentence a sixteen-year-old boy to ten years in prison while claiming to be lenient and kind infuriated me. Since the straps weren't binding me because they couldn't be fastened tightly across my small frame, I felt like leaping out of the chair and bashing that ignorant, cruel judge, and tearing the damned "verdict" into shreds. But I managed to control myself, and without a word let them lead me out toward the unknown prison.

The prison was very big, with eight cell blocks, one of which still stands today—it was the prison for juvenile offenders at Caohejing. I was put into a small cell six feet long by three feet wide. Once inside, I heard the iron door shut behind me with a clang. It was very dark. There were four wooden beds, and in the darkness I could make out three or four figures, thin as ghosts, sizing me up. For the longest time no one spoke. The total silence made my heart sink; I was terrified. Realizing I'd have to spend ten years in this godforsaken place, that I had before me an almost endless string of dark, empty days, my legs grew rubbery and I involuntarily began to sob.

A soft, kind voice then said in my ear, "Why are you crying? What's your name?" Without taking the time to dry my tears, I lifted my head. He was an adult, with a pointed nose, thick lips, and sparkling eyes. In this tiny world, pitch dark and seemingly without hope, it felt warm and comforting to hear a human voice. I looked at him as if he'd just saved my life. "My name is Wang Shouhua."

"Don't cry. Are you a c.y.? A c.y. is a revolutionary, so why are you crying?"*

---

*Author's note: c.y. stands for Communist Youth League.

"I got ten years. And I still don't even know what I did wrong!"

"Just ten years. When you get out of here you'll be three years younger than I am now. When you get out you'll still be a young man, you'll still have time to do something with your life."

I stopped crying then. Later I learned that this twenty-nine-year-old prisoner was Xiao Wenguang, a worker in a Shanghai printing factory in charge of labor union work for the party underground.

In the darkness I heard another man speaking, very softly, in a hoarse voice. Only in a place like this, as quiet as a grave, could you have heard him. "All of us here, whether we've been given ten, eight, or twenty years, are all the same. Some day our Red Army will fight its way to Shanghai. What's more, this prison is in the suburbs and the Guomindang won't be able to hold it. As soon as our Red Army gets here and opens the gates, it'll be like the Bastille gates being thrown open by the flood of the French Revolution in 1789—in one day, all the prisoners were freed, even those sentenced to death."

He spoke with such faith and confidence that I was completely entranced by the beautiful picture he painted. I felt that my imprisonment was only temporary, that it couldn't last too long. I didn't cry anymore, and I recovered my youthful vigor. In that tiny place I began to practice martial arts every day, and I also started to study Japanese. My teacher was Xu Yushu, the man who had talked about the Bastille. He had studied in Japan and spoke fluent Japanese. He said that teaching me Japanese was good for him, too, because he could review the vocabulary he'd otherwise forget.

The biggest problem was the food. They gave us two meals a day. These consisted of boiled rice served in a big, rusty iron pot, on top of which was a small, shallow pot of vegetables. The rice we got was of three types. One kind tasted like it had been burned in a fire. It turned out that a rice warehouse nearby had caught on fire, and after the fire was put out the prison authorities had been able to get the rice for just the price of hauling it away, so they had it brought over to feed us. The second kind was rice that had gone bad. This was old rice that was partially eaten away by maggots, or the dregs swept out of the granaries. When you ate it the foul stench made you lose your appetite. There were lots of cooked maggots in this rice. New inmates were very particular about what they ate, and even used their chopsticks to extract the maggots. One cellmate, Old Zhang, had probably studied nutrition. "When rice maggots are steamed or boiled," he offered, "you can eat them. They're a source of protein, so you don't need to pick them out. Good or bad, they should be treated like a kind of meat." I watched him swallow the maggots without batting an eye, and decided that he made sense. So I began to eat the maggots, too. This fellow, Zhang Yunqing, was a short, sturdily built student from Sichuan.

The third kind of rice tasted of kerosene. The grains were snow-white and large, and, if not for the kerosene taste, would have been high quality. According to our "nutritionist" Zhang Yunqing, this rice was probably imported from Burma or Thailand and had been contaminated by kerosene on the ship bringing it over. The kerosene didn't affect the nutritional value of the rice, so this kind was much better than the other two, since small amounts of kerosene aren't harmful. I just had to hold my nose when I ate it. The funny thing was that our expert, who said we should eat it, couldn't get it down himself. Not without regret, he told us, "Rationally, I know I should eat it, but I just can't. As soon as I smell it I feel like vomiting, and if I throw up everything in my stomach I'll be harming my body more than I would by not eating the rice. So I can't eat it. It's just like a child who won't eat meat. Even if you put the best cut in front of him he won't touch it. There's nothing you can do, because if you force him to eat it he'll throw up. He's stricter in his diet than a Muslim, even."

As for the vegetables in the little pot, they were pretty pitiful. In the winter, for several months in a row, we would get four or five slices of turnip. Chewing those turnips was sometimes like chewing cotton balls, the sole difference being that you could get a bit of a salty taste out of them. In summer for weeks on end we would eat winter melon [a bland vegetable with high water content and little nutritional value]. On rare occasions we would get sweet potato—that was like a first-class banquet for us. My deepest impression is of the time we ate sprouted beans. For prisoners, getting to eat sprouted beans was a once-in-a-lifetime opportunity. According to our "nutritionist," these beans had several kinds of vitamins—the shell contained vitamin C, for instance. We would roll each bean around in our mouths several times before swallowing, and eat it skin and all. For days after we would discuss this delicacy and recall it longingly. Since Old Zhang couldn't eat the kerosene rice, he depended on crackers or cakes sent by his family. In the Guomindang prisons, you were allowed to receive all kinds of food from your family. If you didn't have relatives in Shanghai to bring you anything, you could buy things once a month if you had money saved in the prison "bank," things like peanuts, salted turnips, cookies, and cakes.

Losing your freedom was of course hard to take, but getting food that wasn't even fit for pigs made it worse. The call "time to eat" hardly inspired your appetite here. We ate only because we had to, because we knew we'd be finished if we didn't. So all we could do was force ourselves to swallow the garbage they fed us.

It had been just over a year since I was thrown into this black prison. The beginning of my second year here was when I grew up. Darkness, hunger, and sickness worked on me continuously, tortured me, and changed the appearance of what had been an innocent young boy. I could see my ribs clearly; I could see the curling blood vessels standing out beneath my pale white skin. My gums often bled. I became so thin I didn't even recognize myself.

Xu Yushu didn't approve of my martial arts.

"You're young, you should do a little exercise," he said, "but I don't think you should practice martial arts. We get so little to eat that there just isn't enough nourishment for strenuous exertion."

So I stopped my exercises and poured all my energy into learning Japanese. One day Teacher Xu came to the words for "go out the door" and "go in the door." I froze. Mr. Xu didn't know what was going on. "What's wrong?"

"Those words are useless to me. I won't need them for at least ten years."

He was silent, his eyes moistened with tears.

At dusk one day in late fall, before I'd fallen asleep, I heard the sound of men running around outside the wall. I'd never heard any sound like it before. I leaped out of bed and woke up Xu Yushu, asleep at my feet.

"The Red Army is here!" I shouted. "Listen! It must be the Red Army come to save us!"

My cellmates were all awakened by my shouts. Old Xiao and Old Zhang pressed their ears against the wall and listened carefully to the activity outside. Only Xu Yushu stayed where he was. "The Red Army won't come here," he stated impassively. "They've left Jiangxi and gone far, far away [on their Long March to Yan'an]." He was surely a mysterious man. How did he know that the Red Army had gone far away?

Xiao Wenguang, pressed up against the wall listening, said, "It sounds like they're chasing an escaped prisoner."

"That prisoner is really something!" I exclaimed.

"I'm afraid he won't be able to escape," replied Old Zhang.

"If the Red Army doesn't come soon, I'd also like to try . . . ," I cried.

Xiao Wenguang fixed his gaze on me. "You're out of your mind."

All along I had been relying on what Xu Yushu had said when I first entered this place. Those words had supported me, given me hope. In this miserable little cage I had managed to keep my spirits up, and although I wasn't happy, I had at least managed to avoid worrying. But in that one instant, my hopes were shattered. It was as if the spring inside me which had supplied me with power suddenly snapped. I became completely numb and dejected. I was assailed with all sorts of concerns; I'd practically become an old man overnight. Teacher Xu quickly noticed my change of mood, but said nothing about it. However, one day during my Japanese lesson, he taught me the word for "open the door." I repeated the word eagerly several times, and then asked, "Didn't you say the Red Army was even farther away from here now?"

With a slight smile, he answered, "As long as the Red Army hasn't left China, the day to 'open the door' will come. And I believe that that day is getting closer all the time."

I didn't need to question him further about the basis of his optimistic prediction. Whatever came out of his mouth was gospel to me. His words were my lifeblood. Since he restored my hope, I believed him even more unquestioningly. I've never forgotten the

Japanese word for "open the door," for that word welded back together the spring that had broken inside me.

II

Xu Yushu fell ill, and his legs became swollen. The unanimous diagnosis was beriberi. It was our understanding that if the swelling in the legs gradually spread to the rest of the body, death would quickly follow. The prison medical officer examined him but said nothing. He just left two packets of medicine behind. When we opened them and examined their contents, they turned out to be just chaff and wheat bran. Mr. Xu swallowed this strange, worthless medicine and said, "There's sugar syrup in it. It's got a sweet taste. It's just what I need. The medical officer has also diagnosed it as beriberi."

"The food's been so bad recently, I bet a lot of people will get beriberi," said Old Zhang. "If they don't improve what we eat and only give us chaff and wheat bran for medicine, no one will be able to get over the beriberi."

Everyone began to examine his own legs. Xiao Wenguang pressed his fingers against the backs of his calves and discovered that this left impressions. I tried it too, pressing hard on my calf muscles. Fortunately, the muscles returned to normal right away. "You're lucky you're still young," said Xiao Wenguang. "You can still resist it for a while."

The cell was suddenly filled with the fear of death. We felt the threat of imminent disaster and grew very uneasy, then despondent. I didn't even want to study Japanese anymore, even though the teacher taught me an hour a day as usual. But when I saw that the soles of his feet were inflamed, I couldn't bear to bother him anymore. Unable to stop myself, I grabbed his legs and began to weep. He, on the other hand, calmly encouraged me. "I'm taking medicine. I know this is due to a lack of vitamin B. It'll slowly get better."

Once a week we were allowed to go out for air. We used this time to exchange information with the other political prisoners. Because of Xu Yushu's illness he couldn't go with us. While we were lined up, the other inmates came over and asked with great concern, "Why hasn't Old Xu come out?"

"He's got beriberi and his legs are so swollen you can almost see through them."

"One of our group has it, too."

When we returned to the cell, the four of us told Xu Yushu what we'd learned from the others and conveyed their expressions of concern. Teacher Xu thought it over for a while. "We've got to do something. We have to fight for our lives. We can't wait around to die. The abysmal quality of food is the critical problem."

On June 23, 1935, out of the blue, came a miracle. One afternoon, pieces of soy sauce–braised pork, one for each of us, appeared in the vegetable pot.

When he slid the food into the cell, the guard shouted, "You can thank the new warden Mr. Shao for this favor." We didn't care if the new warden was Zhao, Cao, or whoever. All we cared about was that there was meat, like manna from heaven. When we picked up the little metal pot it felt as if it had gotten much heavier. I hope the reader won't laugh at us—the way we ate the meat wasn't very pretty to look at. I tore my piece in half and held each in my mouth for about fifteen minutes, unwilling to chew it. I thought this was just my own childishness, but I observed that my cellmates, too, were holding the meat in their mouths, pursing their lips, their cheeks bulging. The only difference was that they held it in their mouths for a slightly shorter time, that's all.

"Don't think that this is some great act of mercy," warned Xu Yushu. "No warden is going to use his own money to buy meat for his inmates. In the long run, we'll have to pay for it."

At mealtime the next day I stood by the square opening in the cell door and looked out, waiting for more meat. But I was disappointed. The third day was the same. Mr. Xu knew what a glutton I was, and when I came away empty-handed again the third day, he said, "That piece of meat was just a calling card from the new warden, to make a name for himself. You actually thought he'd give you a piece every day—Little Wang, you're still a child!"

My mouth went dry. I swallowed. "But the guard the other day didn't say anything about only giving us meat that one meal." My cellmates all laughed, whether at my immaturity or my gluttony, I don't know.

Later, Mr. Xu's words proved true. The new warden arrogantly and cruelly did indeed make us pay for our meat. The food began to get worse and worse. There was no longer even any kerosene rice. All we got was rice soaked to the point that only the dregs remained, and for vegetables all we got was "hollow vegetable" [water convolvulus, or bindweed], which you could chew forever to no avail. All we could do was pick it out and throw it away. "They should use this stuff to make the shafts for writing brushes." "The name is certainly apt; you can't eat it at all, it's completely hollow."

Under these conditions, the beriberi began to spread.

III

"We have to struggle for our survival," repeated Xu Yushu. "If things continue like this, we'll never get out of here alive."

But what method of struggle should we adopt? A fast—a collective hunger strike!

The next time we went out for air we presented this new "proposal" to the other prisoners, one by one. And we established signals by which we could communicate. I still remember them. To knock on the wall three times in a row meant you agreed to carry out the strike; five times in succession meant that the strike was to begin from the meal just being served; to knock twice, stop, and knock twice again meant that we were to resume eating. Our cell became the command center. The initial three knocks came from the other cells to us, and the other signals went from our cell to the others. This indicated that the other prisoners were awaiting our instructions. That night we got a lot of signals from the other cells.

"Everyone supports our proposal," said Xu Yushu, "so let's go ahead. But before we can begin, we have to prepare." By preparing, he meant for each cell to store emergency provisions. Some cells didn't have enough provisions, so others distributed some of their stock to them. In this sense, we were carrying out something very similar to primitive communism.

So, the decision was made. The atmosphere suddenly became tense and earnest. It was quiet as usual, but you could see from their faces that each man was preparing himself for a life-and-death struggle.

Because I was so young, and since this was to be my first hunger strike, my "big brothers" took special care of me and gave me a lot of encouragement. "A Communist Party member in the enemy's prison has to struggle with the Guomindang, even if he has no weapons," said Old Zhang. "A hunger strike is our only weapon."

"Fasting for several days is quite arduous," said Xiao Wenguang, "but you can do it if you grit your teeth, keep your spirits high, and maintain the will to fight. Last year in late fall we went on a hunger strike. We fasted for four days and were victorious in the end. In the beginning every prisoner sentenced to five years or more had his legs bound in chains. But because of the strike the Guomindang had to give in and take them off."

We began storing up water. Then each of us put the provisions sent by his family into our group stock and divided everything into five portions. Guo Shouqi contributed the most. That month he'd bought more than a pound of fried peanuts, which he hadn't eaten yet. He also had six or seven sesame cakes stored up. And Xiao Wenguang contributed a ricecake and half a jar of peanuts. Because I didn't have any family in Shanghai, I had nothing to contribute. I felt terrible about this, because I'd be eating other people's food.

All day we busied ourselves with careful preparations. We counted the peanuts one by one and divided the total by five—each of us getting 137 peanuts. We carefully calculated how many slices of ricecake there were—each of us getting 34.

That night we were excited and tense. Everyone held his breath, either unwilling or unable to sleep.

"With this small amount of material preparation we can carry on the struggle for quite some time," said Teacher Xu.

"It's too bad I didn't know about our strike earlier," said Guo Shouqi, "or I could have had my family bring us more food; then we would have been a little better prepared."

"Don't eat any of these things the first two days," advised Old

Zhang, our "nutritionist." "You should wait until the third day to begin eating them."

But Xu Yushu disagreed. "Each person's physical constitution is different. Some may not be able to make it to the third day. In that case, it's all right to eat a little of your portion before then."

Though I had never experienced hunger for days on end, I wasn't at all nervous. I saw the pouch near my pillow filled with my portion of provisions; there were peanuts, ricecakes, and sesame cakes. I didn't have to eat that rotten rice and useless "hollow vegetable" anymore, and the idea of a hunger strike sure beat not doing anything.

We gave the sign for the strike. The cell was exceptionally quiet and solemn. You could feel the tension in the air. The time for the morning meal came. We peered out the hole of the cell door and saw that the other cells had refused to accept any food. When it was our turn to be fed, Old Zhang was standing watch at the door. "Please tell the warden that the food situation is unbearable," he said to the guard. "There's not enough of it, and all we get is 'hollow vegetable,' which is so hard you can't even chew it; we never get any oil, and several prisoners have contracted beriberi. We ask the new warden to respond to our demands."

The guard rapped the door with his hand and said, "You're striking too? You won't eat?"

"We protest that the warden is pocketing part of the money allocated for our food!"

The guard was stunned for a moment, then reacted, "So you've all arranged this beforehand?" With this, he walked to the door of the next cell.

All thirty-eight cells struck. At ten o'clock the gates of the two cells at the entrance were opened. We heard a lot of footsteps, then a voice called out, "Are you going to eat or not? If you won't eat such good food, we'll let you enjoy the taste of a beating instead!"

Other voices shouted, "Move, move. You can tell your story to the section head!"

It seemed that several prisoners were dragged out. An hour later we heard the sound of more than a few of them reentering the cell row, slowly dragging thick, noisy ankle shackles behind them. One of them deliberately shouted loudly, "If you don't respond to our demands, beating us and chaining our legs won't do you any good! We'll hold out till the end!" His voice was so resonant and strong that inmates in all thirty-eight cells could hear him.

Xu Yushu was upset but also pleased. He nodded his head, "That was clearly Li Huchen, I can tell his voice. They've been beaten up for sure."

"The authorities will be severe since they've just taken over," said Xiao Wenguang. "During last year's strike they did the same thing as soon as we began."

The first day all we had was a little water, nothing else. By evening I began to feel hungry. But I tightened my belt buckle and lay down very early, just staring at the ceiling. After a while I got tired and fell asleep.

The second day I woke up very early, probably because of my hunger pangs. Fortunately, I had my emergency rations next to my pillow. I reached in, grabbed some peanuts and counted out twenty. I put one in my mouth, which had a wonderful taste, and held it there as long as I could. I spent five or six minutes on each one. Ah, those beautiful peanuts! They were the elixir of life, they were lifesaving pills. Having eaten all twenty, I took stock—my store was visibly reduced. If I ate twenty each time, six more meals and my 137 peanuts would be gone! I regretted my action and was angry at myself for not listening to "nutritionist" Zhang Yunqing's advice to wait until the third day.

A hungry man pays particular notice to his neighbor's mouth, observing him with unusual acuteness and sensitivity. I discovered that Old Zhang, lying motionless on his wooden bed, also seemed to have something in his mouth. So now I had found a way to rationalize my error, and I felt better. No matter what, though, those twenty peanuts I'd eaten were gone forever.

The third day of the strike began. According to Old Zhang, this was the crucial day, and it was all right to eat a little more. I was terribly hungry, and in the morning I ate half a sesame cake. To my dismay, the cake seemed to increase my appetite, and I couldn't help departing from my original plan. I began to nibble at the edges of the second half, like a silkworm working away at the edges of his precious mulberry leaf. Gradually the cake stopped resembling a half-moon and took on the shape of a thinner and thinner crescent. When there was only a thin crescent left, I began to get upset, for I was eating two days' worth of food in one sitting. What would I do later on? That afternoon I ate twenty more peanuts and drank a lot of water. By nightfall I was still hungry. I told my cellmates how I was feeling, and Xiao Wenguang criticized me. "Remember, from now on no one is allowed to talk about how hungry he is, or to say that something tastes good." There was nothing I could say.

The even more sophisticated "nutritionist" Zhang Yunqing admonished us. "Remember, no one should talk unnecessarily. Moving your lips and tongue consumes calories. . . . What I just said probably burned over a peanut's worth of calories." Everyone laughed, but Old Zhang remained very serious, not even cracking a smile. Perhaps laughing consumed calories too.

That afternoon the medical officer came and went through the motions of checking blood pressure, listening to hearts, and feeling foreheads. "You're destroying your own bodies," he said in a sympathetic voice. "What's the point? Tell me your demands and I'll go speak to the warden. If you keep striking you'll all get sick, and I'll be too busy to help anyone."

Teacher Xu told him, "Please report to the new warden that we have four demands: we won't eat bad rice; we want better vegetables and oil in the vegetables; we want a piece of meat each week; and we want permission to read magazines and journals."

The medical officer nodded. "I'll tell him."

Old Zhang sat up from his bed. His forehead was beaded with sweat. "No more beating and abusing the prisoners. The shackles put on during the strike must be taken off!"

"All right, I'll tell him."

That night I was too hungry to sleep. I had eaten quite a bit that day, so why was I still so hungry? There was nothing to be done—I reached into my bag and pulled out a peanut. It tasted wonderful, but I couldn't help taking another and another. . . . Once I began I couldn't stop; I don't know how many I ate.

The strike entered the fourth day. We didn't know whether or not the medical officer had reported our demands. It seemed as if the new warden had resolved to hold firm and not meet our terms. There was no activity that day, except that the authorities gave each cell two extra pots of water.

That day was really the end of the line for me. When I got up I counted my peanuts. The previous night's "orgy" had reduced my store of 137 to 26. There were only 34 slices of ricecake left. By noon of that day, not only had I eaten all the peanuts, but I'd even finished off the ricecake. As I was pulling off the slices I had a strange notion. "The baker had been overzealous in slicing the ricecake," I thought. "Each slice is equally thin. Why didn't that damned baker slice some of them a little thicker!"

Now I had to face the coming days with an empty bag; I had eaten the last of my provisions.

That afternoon, the fourth day, was the worst. I can still remember the taste. My mouth kept secreting saliva, very bitter saliva. But when I went to spit it out I found my mouth was actually dry. The bitter taste was coming from the coating on my tongue. I also felt the emptiness in my stomach begin to spread to my spine. This confirms the Chinese saying, "the belly is so empty that it spreads to the spine." This expression comes from experience; it's no exaggeration. What does it feel like? If you haven't been through this kind of hunger yourself, it's almost impossible to comprehend. Basically, it feels like your whole body is about to disintegrate any minute; it feels like your legs are floating, suspended in mid-air, and you don't know where you're floating to. The strange thing was that my brain wasn't affected at all by the hunger. It kept working away, and in fact seemed to be working harder than ever. My head remained clear throughout, and I was immediately aware of every sound and every disturbance outside. Unfortunately, this meant that the hunger, too, was particularly sharp, and this made it impossible to escape the pain.

IV

The fifth day approached slowly, terribly slowly. But finally it arrived. My more experienced cellmates said that last year the hunger strike ended in victory on the fourth day. But this new warden wanted to test his strength against ours and was unwilling to compromise. No one knew what happened when you went hungry for five days. I observed the movements of the others and noticed that Old Zhang still had some peanuts left. When he finished off the last one he heaved a weak and regretful sigh. His forehead oozed large beads of sweat. Xiao Wenguang's beriberi began to act on his legs. The way he staved off the hunger was to hold some water in his mouth to try to make himself feel as if he were eating something. I noticed that Teacher Xu was eating his last slice of ricecake. His face was as ashen as a piece of white paper, and his eyes were shut tight. If not for the faint movement of his mouth you might have thought he was dead. Taking in this frightful scene, I grew quite disheartened. Guo Shouqi was also lying there as still as a corpse, letting the sunlight from the window shine on him. He looked like a statue of a sage. I saw something in his mouth, too, and it didn't look like water. I was envious, even jealous, that he had something in his mouth. I thought that if he still had something to eat he must be the happiest person in the world. I hated myself, cursed myself as worthless and without self-control because I'd finished all my food so quickly. Who knew how long the hunger strike would last? As I was thinking this, I suddenly noticed something white pop out of Guo Shouqi's mouth. It was a little ball and it went rolling onto the floor. Old Guo didn't move a muscle, as if to say, "Let it go." I felt uneasy. The small ball gave rise to an uncontrollable appetite, and I fixed my eyes on it greedily, fearing it might roll away or be eaten by a rat. I mustered all my strength and began to get up. My whole body was weak, my bones felt soft, and my mind grew cloudy. Thousands of stars danced before my eyes. Old Zhang was very concerned. "What are you doing?"

I lied. "I have to take a leak." The fact was, since I hadn't eaten or drunk anything for days, I didn't have the need to relieve myself.

I got off the bed and picked up Old Guo's little white ball. I felt like I had picked up a tiny life. Just then I heard a heavy dragging sound in the hall outside the cell. This was the sound we'd always heard at mealtime just before they served the food.

"The warden is giving you meat—one piece of braised pork apiece!" shouted a guard. "Quickly, get up and eat!" He sounded like a shopkeeper hollering about a sale. Behind the guard were two inmates from the kitchen staff, dragging several pots. Xu Yushu opened his eyes and said weakly, "Little Wang, go take a look." With great difficulty I staggered over to the door and looked out the hole. The pots really did contain beautiful, sweet-smelling pieces of braised pork. I couldn't help from shouting, "We've won! Let's eat this beautiful meal!" I threw away the little white ball I'd been holding in my hand. There were beads of cold sweat on my forehead, but my spirit hadn't broken. I was still able to move if I held onto the bed for support.

Xu Yushu was unusually cool. "This is a trick," he said. "They're trying to use a piece of meat to break our resolve. We're striking for four demands, and we'll eat only after the warden has responded to each of them. Don't pay attention to them, Little Wang, don't pay attention."

Old Zhang added, "We've starved for five days for what? A lousy piece of meat? We have to keep going until we win."

Resentfully, I left the cell door—my joy and the appetite that had just been stirred up completely dissipated. Now I recalled the little ball I'd thrown away, and after a long search I finally found it, picked it up, and used my handkerchief to clean it off, preparing to put it in my mouth. It was only then that I realized what the ball was—the chewed-up wrapper from a ricecake. Hoping that it still had some of the sweet flavor, Guo Shouqi had sucked it into a ball. What taste or nutritional value would it have now? I threw it away. At that moment the hunger pangs and the despair that I felt were worse even than moments before, when I'd stood at the door and seen the meat and realized I wouldn't be able to eat it. I lay down on the hard wooden bed. Thousands of golden stars played before my eyes again. I closed them to try to get rid of the stars, which confused and exhausted me. Suddenly, the scene changed on the "screen" before my eyes and there were no more stars. Instead, there was a beautiful, glistening, sweet-smelling piece of pork. I could even see the steam coming off it. This mirage was even more enticing than the real thing, and more harmful. It was as if my whole body had turned into a steaming piece of meat. When I pressed my fingers together they felt greasy and oily; when I opened my eyes, even the water stains on the ceiling resembled pieces of gleaming pork; my ears were full of the sound of pots being dragged along the floor announcing "time to eat." I tried as hard as I could to stop all these tortuous images, but to no avail.

Why not try Xiao Wenguang's tactic of keeping water in the mouth? It had to be better than nothing. So I began to struggle to my feet for the second time, planning to use my teacup to get some water. As I started to drag myself up I put my hand out on the sheet beside my pillow and bumped into something hard. I pulled away the sheet and discovered a true miracle: a real, actual sesame cake. This was no illusion, it really was a sesame cake! Where had it come from? Heaven? Could it really have come from heaven to save me?

How fantastic! What timing! But why hadn't I noticed it earlier? A sesame cake was worth 50 peanuts; no, not just 50, even 100 peanuts don't equal one sesame cake. Having no time to think about it, I picked it up and took a bite. It was sweet and light and had that wonderful sesame flavor. I regretted, though, that my first bite had been too greedy. I should treasure it, chew it slowly. Who could say how long the strike would continue? Now the mirage of braised meat no longer haunted me. Was this not materialism triumphing over the challenge of stream of consciousness?

It was only after I'd eaten the first bite that I realized that just popping it into my mouth like that, without first finding out where it came from, was not a very honorable thing to do. By contrast, Old Guo had contributed all of his food to the group, then got back the same portion as everyone else; just a little while ago he was silently chewing on a cake wrapper. I hadn't contributed a thing to the group but still got a full portion. Yet when I found this cake of uncertain origin, which hadn't been included in the original calculation, I ate it secretly. How could I have eaten it? This was more shameful than committing a crime. I was unable to take another bite.

Turning the half-eaten cake over and over in my hand, I said, "I've just found an extra sesame cake. Whose is it?"

Xu Yushu lifted his head from the pillow with great difficulty. "It's all right. I still have some."

It was only then that I realized that when I had gone over to the cell door Old Xu had secretly placed the cake under my sheet. He picked up the two packets of medicine lying near his pillow. "This medicine of mine is as good as food. You're young, you can't go without food. . . . You eat the cake." Tears began to flow down my cheeks in torrents, dripping onto the sesame cake in my hand. A feeling of warmth and love filled my whole being, but I could think of nothing to say to express how I felt.

Twice during the afternoon of the fifth day the medical officer had to be rushed in to treat emergency cases in neighboring cells. Due to starvation and weak constitutions, two comrades had gone into shock from heart failure. The atmosphere in our cell once again filled with tension and terror. Teacher Xu, Xiao Wenguang, and Guo Shouqi, all weak and pale, looked like they too could go into shock at any moment. But there was no chance, I felt, of my having heart failure. Since I had eaten that extra sesame cake, my strength and spirits were vastly improved. It was as if the two-ounce piece of cake had snatched me from the jaws of death. Perhaps it was the two inmates' going into shock that broke the warden's resolve. At four o'clock that afternoon, two head guards brought a notice from him, which they read loudly several times: "In response to prisoners' requests, we are going to improve the quality of the food; supply better quality rice; add one piece of meat each week . . . "

"Wasn't there one more demand?"

"What demand?"

"Allowing us to read magazines and journals."

"That one isn't on the list," he said. "I'm afraid the special municipal [Guomindang] party office won't agree. But the warden has already spoken with the educational officials. We will allow your relatives to bring in any journals you want, as long as they're legal publications."

Mr. Xu's face took on a little color. He smiled. I tearfully embraced him, shouting happily, "We won! We won!"

Mr. Xu pushed me from him. "Spread the word quickly. Knock on the wall and tell everyone we can eat again!"

"What do I do? I forget how to give the signal."

"Knock twice, stop, then twice again. I don't have the strength to knock. You do it!'' he said weakly, but with great excitement. And so I was entrusted with this glorious mission. I summoned up my strength, went over to the left-hand wall, and knocked loudly. When I finished I went and knocked at the right side. Perhaps it was because of that last sesame cake that my knocking was so loud. It was like a military drum beating out the sound of victory, it was like giving the signal that life had won out over death. At that point I had suddenly become the commander, with control over the fates of all the other inmates. It was the first time in my life that I reveled in the joyous taste of victory, the sweet flavor of revolutionary struggle!

Two years later, the Anti-Japanese War broke out. Under pressure from the people of the whole country, the Guomindang released us [due to the Guomindang–CCP united front against the Japanese]. What Xu Yushu had said my first day in prison had come true. Regardless of their sentences—ten years, eight years, or life imprisonment—all inmates received their freedom within the space of a few days.

Most of the men released from that black hole headed for the revolutionary center in the Northwest—Yan'an. Some went to northern Jiangsu and became the vanguard in establishing the anti-Japanese base there.

Hunger Trilogy

Part 2

I

IN SEPTEMBER 1942 I was working in the Bohai Region of the Shandong base. There were rumors that the Japanese devils and troops of Chinese traitors had gathered in the Qingzhou area along the train line between Jinan and Jiaoxian. To prepare the resistance against their mop-up operation, the units in our military region reduced their number of nonmilitary personnel. Some comrades and I were organized into a small group, which included an older man named Zhang Chuanhe and a woman named Wang Lei, who had just come from Jinan. She had moved heaven and earth to ascertain that her high school sweetheart had joined the Eighth Route Army, and she had figured out a way to come to the Bohai liberated area to look for him. She finally found him, but before they had a chance for a real talk word came that there would soon be fighting, and that she was to be included in the ranks of the evacuated personnel sent to the rear. I remember there was also somebody else, a college student from Anhui named Hong Ling, and some others—injured soldiers and old or sick—nine people in all.

Zhang Chuanhe was the leader of our group. He was from Huimin County in the Bohai Region and had taught elementary school for several years when he was young. He wore thick glasses for nearsightedness, and it was because of this that he was a member of the group of injured soldiers and old and sick. It was quite a task for Zhang Chuanhe to bring together this group of nine people, all strangers from different posts. His first

25

order was that no one could carry more than six pounds of personal effects. The second was to issue each person a bag for dry rations, such as flour biscuits and buns. An older, experienced member of the group added some advice: don't forget to carry a small package of salt.

This was Wang Lei's first time in an anti-Japanese base area away from the enemy-occupied city, so everything was new to her. When she heard that we were going to fight the Japanese, she was excited, curious, and frightened. Whatever she was ordered to do she did thoroughly; the only thing she had a problem with was reducing the amount of goods she carried. She had come from Jinan, and the things she brought to give her boyfriend must have weighed at least twenty-five pounds. She'd intended to hand all of it over to him, but in his rush to return to his unit he couldn't carry a thing, so it was all left with Wang Lei. Each and every item represented the crystallization of her love and concern for him: how could she bear to give them up? But in the end, swallowing her pain, she gave the shoes, hot water bottle, enamel wash basin, and other things to a villager's elder daughter.

The air suddenly grew tense when word came that the Japanese devils, six or seven thousand strong, had already crossed the Xiaoqing River and were about to begin a mop-up operation in the Bohai Region. That night we ate our fill of dinner and prepared to march with the rear service segments of the attached units in the general direction of Guangbei (the northern part of Guangrao County). Our small detachment of nine, under the leadership of Zhang Chuanhe, was ready and waiting. His expression stern and tense, Zhang inspected the ration bag each of us wore around the neck. The ration bag was, in fact, just a double-layered cloth bag stuffed with biscuits. It looked like a little white dragon. Zhang also inspected the weight of our backpacks, but in a haphazard way, just by measuring with his eyes. Because he was so nearsighted, he didn't notice that Wang Lei's backpack was far overweight.

A whistle blew, and the large force moved out. We didn't ask where we were going and didn't worry about how far the enemy would get; all we knew was to follow the horses and men in the large force.

We followed the force for two days to avoid the spearhead of the Japanese attack, and we had already made several circles on the great plain of Bohai Bay. We were sure the enemy would withdraw to Jinan. But on the third day worse news arrived: the Japanese forces had divided into two battalions and set out from Shouguang County to launch a surprise attack against the Bohai military command units. An emergency order required rear service units to disperse to reduce the size of the target. Each small unit was to fight independently for more flexibility and make its way separately to the Lijinwa area to settle down in concealment.

When the unit consisting of just the nine of us left the main force and began marching through the vast, seemingly limitless countryside, we felt lonely and empty, like a child separated from its mother.

"Our superiors want us to go to Lijinwa to hide," said Zhang Chuanhe. "That's really a good place, and the Japanese have never gone there. Let's go!" We were fortunate to have a leader familiar with local conditions. After being separated from the main force, all we could do was pin our hopes on Zhang.

As our small unit moved northeast, the farther we went, the fewer villages we encountered. And each village had only four or five families. When we grew tired, it was with great difficulty that we located a village at which to catch our breath, drink some water, and eat some of our rations. But this village had no drinking well, only a shallow well with bitter, brackish water. We asked an old villager what they ordinarily drank. "Every week or two we go to a place some seven miles away and carry back buckets of drinking water," said the old man. "And during the rainy season we use barrels, basins, bowls, and gourds to catch the water that the old man in heaven sends down." All we could do was purse our dry, wizened lips and make do without. We asked the old villager how far it was to Lijinwa. The old man pointed north. "That's a desolate area I've never been across. From here going northeast, you probably have two days' walk."

In low spirits, the nine of us doggedly walked northeasterly. The great plain of Bohai Bay is a lousy place. No trees grow there, just desolate earth—you don't see a single crow or sparrow. Strictly speaking there were no "roads" there, because the whole area was wasteland. I understand that in ancient times the Yellow River flowed through there on its way to the sea, but now, after changing course, the river left behind this solid wasteland. Any way you wanted to go you could go; the land looked as though it had been pressed down by a giant roller. It was flat and hard except for occasional blades of reddish grass. If our soccer, basketball, or volleyball teams wanted to build a soccer field here, or a basketball or volleyball court, they could make it as big as they wanted!

We kept walking and walking on this interminable plain. Wang Lei's backpack was getting heavier and heavier, so after a painful struggle, she made up her mind to get rid of more of her things. We stopped and watched her open the large pack on her back and the small one in front. We saw then that her "equipment" was completely inappropriate for wartime, and all the more so for a long-distance march, for she was still carrying a coffee pot, a big round mirror that weighed over two pounds, and four different brushes: a shoe brush, a clothes brush, a wash brush, and a hair brush. Her cosmetics had already been reduced to a minimum, but there were still four or five kinds, weighing over a pound. Some of the other things looked like decorations for newlyweds: a matching pair of enamel ashtrays and soap dishes, several sets of embroidered pillow cases, large pajamas. . . . All of these things reflected her great care for and unswerving loyalty toward her fiancé. They seemed to have formed a part of her life, and the reason she was unwilling to part with them was that they were the fruits of her painstaking efforts, of her aspirations for love and happiness.

Now, with blushing face and aching heart, she was going to dump this lovely "dowry" in the middle of this bleak no-man's land. Why was she embarrassed? She had not obeyed Zhang's orders, as evidenced by her now fully displayed items. Second, to display publicly all these bright and colorful objects was rather awkward for a young girl who wanted with all her might to keep her love a secret. If I had been a big husky guy with the muscle to shoulder a heavy load, I would have liked to carry those things for her—I couldn't bear to get rid of them either.

Wang Lei had carried her load a hundred miles, and the weight of it had almost bent her at the waist. The endless path lying before us strengthened her resolve to dump the stuff. "If I can find my love," she thought, "it won't matter if I have these with me or not."

Once she had made her decision, she grew considerably more relaxed. Zhang Chuanhe praised her. "This is a rare revolutionary act, a symbol of your separation from the old life and the wants of the petty bourgeoisie." "But," he added, "since you couldn't carry this stuff, why didn't you leave it with someone earlier? Wouldn't it have been good to give it to the old villager?"

She blushed again. "I couldn't make the decision then. By the time I couldn't carry it any longer we'd already reached this awful place. You can walk ten miles here without coming across a single villager."

Our small unit again headed north; before we had gotten very far Zhang Chuanhe turned and looked back. He saw Wang Lei's discarded mirror reflecting brilliant rays of light in the middle of the wilderness. He ordered everyone to stop and then ran back by himself, carefully covering up the mirror with dirt and weeds. He ran back, panting for breath. "We almost made a serious mistake. That mirror gives off a bright reflection; if spotted, it would give Japanese planes a nice target!"

Wang Lei explained her action. "My idea was to attract passersby so they would pick these things up. That would be better than throwing them away."

"Unit leader Zhang's caution is unwarranted," said Hong Ling. "This is a deserted area. If a Japanese plane sees the light and the men grow suspicious, circle the area, and drop bombs or spray it with machine gun fire, the joke will be on them because they will have wasted fuel and ammunition!''

''And what if they harm our people or livestock?'' refuted Zhang Chuanhe.

''We'll be long gone by then,'' replied Hong Ling.

I fully agreed with him. Here we were, worried that we had no way to deal with the Japanese bandits, and now we could play a joke on them—how fantastic! Hong proved himself worthy of his college education by coming up with an idea like this.

Zhang Chuanhe, Wang Lei, and the others all looked back at the spot, and then, as if on cue, up at the blue sky. Zhang was won over. ''He's right. Their bombs will just add a few holes if dropped here. Later when they really attack our troops, they'll be short a few bombs. This'll be a good contribution to the anti–mop-up effort.''

Volunteering for the job, I ran back to the spot where the mirror was buried and uncovered it so it lay flat under the sky; I also took advantage of the opportunity to look at the reflection of my thin face, alive with mischief.

After we had walked far, far away, we could still see the reflection from the mirror. I wished that at that moment a Japanese plane would have flown over the area so I could have seen the devils fall for our trick.

II

Wang Lei had never imagined the mirror would turn out to be so useful after all. Thus, she no longer had to feel bad about her pile of discards. In fact, she even felt a bit proud. And since her pack was suddenly ten to fifteen pounds lighter, she looked like a soldier ''entering battle with a light pack.''

We continued in the wilderness, walking and walking, until we saw ahead of us what seemed to be a splendid manor. The high roof of a church was also visible. ''Who would build a church in a place like this?'' exclaimed Hong Ling. ''They have to have a drinking well there,'' I said.

But when we rushed up to the site, the beautiful manor was no longer there. Zhang Chuanhe took off his glasses and then put them back on—still nothing there. He figured it was his bad eyesight. But then he suddenly understood. "I'm afraid what we just saw was a mirage,"

"A mirage is an illusion that appears at sea. This sure isn't the sea," said Hong Ling.

"On a plain sometimes you can see a mirage," insisted Zhang.

After acknowledging that what we'd just seen was indeed a mirage, the nine of us were like a deflated ball. We moved forward, listlessly. But it was painful to move even a step. We slouched down on top of our packs, disheartened and silent. The gathering nightfall gradually grew gray and dark, and the fall wind was chilly. All around us was nothing but bare field without vegetation. "Where are we fleeing to, anyway?" Old Xue asked Zhang.

"We don't have a mission to fight," Zhang responded. "If we can keep ourselves alive and well during the anti–mop-up campaign, we'll have accomplished our mission."

Hong Ling asserted, "There's not a village for miles around, no sign of human life. We're separated from the people and don't even have any way to get a drink of water. I think we should resist the mop-up campaign together with the peasants."

"Weren't we given orders to separate and head for Lijinwa? Let's head straight there," decided Old Zhang.

"Since that's a good place to scatter and hide our forces," I said, "and we've been walking for several days, why haven't we come across any of our brother units?" My unexpected question carried a lot of force. Everyone was silent for a while. "I say we stop going north," said Hong Ling. "I suggest we figure out a way to return to the old base."

"What's Lijinwa like, do you know?" Old Xue asked Zhang.

"It's a primeval forest, many miles around. Refugees from southern and central Shandong have gathered there—it's a reliable mass base," said Old Zhang. He paused, then added,

"That's what I've heard, anyway. I've never been there myself."

"Now that our group is exhausted, what should our course be from here on? We have to develop a plan. We can't afford to delay; we're no unit of young, strong commandos," said Old Xue.

Pained, Zhang clenched his teeth. "Since the party entrusted the eight of you to my charge, I will be responsible for you. Let's do this: it's late already. Let's find a place to camp for the night and we'll decide tomorrow, after we get some clearer information."

It was already so dark you couldn't see your hand in front of your face. How could we look for a place to pitch camp? Several people reached into their bags for biscuits, but the moisture in them had completely evaporated, making them hard as rocks. Our already parched mouths were burning, so even if we could have chewed the biscuits we couldn't have swallowed them.

"Hey! Look—there are lights over there!" Someone had discovered lights glimmering far in the distance. Everyone looked in the direction he was pointing and, sure enough, there were spots of light looking like soy beans in the distance.

I calculated the lights to be about ten miles away, north and a bit west. On a plain you can see particularly far, and things that seem close can take forever to reach. I didn't tell the others my estimate because I was afraid it would dampen their spirits.

Attracted by this tiny bit of light, nine people once again braced themselves and headed for the lights. There lay the water I wanted to drink, the steaming rice I wanted to eat, and a bed I could lie on. There lay everything we wished for with all our hearts.

Eventually, we reached the lights. The owner of the dwelling had just opened the reed door of his home when we all sank to the ground, completely exhausted. His accent confirmed what Zhang had said that day about there being a lot of refugees from southern and central Shandong. But there were only two families in this "residential area," the families of two brothers. They had come from a mountainous area in southern Shandong, where they had been so poor that they had no roof over their heads and not an inch of land. All the land there was owned already, mostly by a big landlord. The two brothers had had enough of the landlord's abuse and resolved to find a piece of land of their own. They had wandered far and wide, ending up here. This land was barren and unoccupied. It had a rock-hard, alkaline soil that produced only white powder. But relying on their youth and strength and over ten years of gritty, determined effort, they had created a small, fertile oasis.

The four-room house was made of twigs and branches. The roof was covered over with the creeping vines of gourds and beans. They had more than ten chickens, and a yellow dog.

No one at all used to come visit them, but now, all of a sudden, lots of people were showing up. Some had traveled a hundred miles or more, paying a visit to their house in the middle of the night. The owner of the house appeared to be overwhelmed by this unexpected attention. The old yellow dog had never seen so much action, either, and he went around sniffing everybody's shoes and backpacks, gleefully wagging his tail with an air of warm welcome.

The peasant's wife put water on to boil for us, steamed our dry rations, and even cooked a pot of potatoes. Fresh water was equally precious here, since they had to go four or five miles for it. According to the peasant, the fresh water didn't come from a well, but from a low-lying bog. A tiny bit of fresh water flowed into the bog from somewhere, and in the space of twenty-four hours they could get enough to fill their earthenware pot. Old Zhang offered that since it was so hard to get water, we'd go there the next day and carry a few buckets back. "You don't need to go," said the peasant. "Even if you went, you wouldn't be able to carry any back. It takes about three or four days before you can scoop out two bucketfuls." Thus there was no way for us to carry out the Eighth Route Army's good tradition of filling up someone's water barrel if you stay in his house. We felt embarrassed about drinking their water, which they had so painstakingly accumulated. We had also eaten their potatoes, so Old Zhang took out two one-dollar "Beihai" notes, but the peasant adamantly refused to take any money. He was very interested in the notes, though, for they were new to him. "We haven't used paper money for many years." Old Zhang insisted on giving him money, so, embarrassed, the man accepted one of the bills. He rubbed it over and over. "Don't they use the central government's notes anymore out there?" With a little smile, Old Zhang explained, "In the Shandong base area now, everyone uses Beihai notes, the currency of the Communist Party. It's the only cash you can buy things with. For a long time now the central government's money has been useless."

"So the Communist Party has its own currency," remarked the old villager, looking at the money. "I'll keep it, but not to buy anything. This is a generous gift you're leaving me."

Old Zhang asked him where Lijinwa was, and what it was like there, and if other units of the Eighth Route Army had gone there. "This whole plain is Lijinwa; the woods you're talking about are four or five miles north of here. As for the Eighth Route Army, this is our first encounter!"

"Have the Japanese been to those woods?" asked Old Zhang.

The villager shook his head. "No. If they did go in, it would be a great trap. They'd never come out."

At daybreak the next day we stood on high ground looking north and did indeed see a thick, dense forest of green and gray. After a discussion, we decided that it would still be safest to go into the woods to conceal ourselves. If we stayed in this little village of two families, and the Japanese mop-up operation reached here, the nine of us would have a hard time hiding ourselves. If we marched in this vast plain without hills or trees for cover, we'd never escape the enemy's pursuit. So we parted from the kind brothers and headed north. The old yellow dog followed right behind us for a long way, and we had a hard time driving him back.

III

Having had our fill of that bare landscape, having walked enough on that white, rock-hard plain, when we reached the edge of the green, luxuriant woods we felt a sensation of freshness, as if we had arrived on another planet. We felt like we were starting a new endeavor. Even the air was different here: it was a very attractive fragrance mingled with a slightly damp and moldy scent, which somewhat resembled the smell of distilled sorghum wine.

Only after we entered the woods did we realize that though Old Zhang had been calling this "a great forest," it turned out he was terribly wrong.

From a distance this vast stretch did look like a forest of trees. The fact was, there wasn't a single tree in it. What grew here was a kind of shrub, about ten feet tall, with twigs about as thick as your two thumbs. The landscape was the result of hundreds of years of silt deposit left after the Yellow River changed course. The great mass of bushes illustrated the power of nature. But anyone who came here had to ask himself why there was only one kind of vegetation, and why it had grown so uniformly.

Old Zhang sighed. "Hearing about something just isn't the same as seeing it for yourself. How could this place be considered a great forest? But it's very dense, a good place for concealment."

We entered the wooded area, following a little path where the shrubs had been cut. Wang Lei was wearing a pair of rubber shoes, bouncing along on the earth, soft under its covering of fallen leaves. Happily, she sang, ". . . everywhere in the dense wood that one treads, there's a place for the comrades to rest their heads." Old Zhang was relieved to have gotten us to this perfect sanctuary, and he finally relaxed. "Maybe we'll run into our comrades from the rear guard units."

We were inspired by this tempting prospect and with a burst of energy pushed forward. The bright sunshine no longer reached us; the sky was completely blocked by the thick branches and leaves, and we felt cool and comfortable. We didn't come across a single comrade from the Eighth Route Army—all we saw were two wild rabbits who scampered in front of us and then rapidly disappeared in the brush.

We continued until we got hungry, then sat down to eat.

Chomping away on his hard steamed bun, Hong Ling commented to Zhang Chuanhe, "We're not an exploration unit, why do we have to keep going forward? You think the Japanese can reach us here?"

Hong Ling made sense, but Zhang disagreed. "We're better off going in a little farther. You ought to know, the Japanese are barbaric."

"We've left the main body of our forces and don't know anything," I said. "We also don't know how far the Japanese troops have advanced. All we know is to keep heading northeast. We've come to a dead end in this huge woods; maybe we should stop and send somebody out to make contact. After we've gotten in touch with our unit we can decide what to do next."

"My job is to guarantee the safety of the eight of you," rejoined Zhang. "If we send somebody out to make contact, what do we do if he gets separated and runs into a problem? You're all intellectuals; you don't understand war and don't have any concept of the enemy. We have to think about the enemy with every move we make; they're sly and barbaric!"

Neither Hong Ling nor I said another word. But Wang Lei interjected, "We came to fight the devils, not to hide from them. If I'd known before that it would be like this, I would have gladly gone to the front." She was so earnest and enthusiastic, I wanted to laugh but couldn't.

Believing in democracy, Zhang Chuanhe finally made a decision. "Let's first find a place to make camp on the edge of the woods. If we come across any sign of the enemy, we'll head in deeper for cover. In a few days Old Wang and I will go out to look for our forces."

After we finished eating, the nine of us hurried back out. We ran and ran, but couldn't tell if we were leaving the same way we'd come in. Zhang was confident. "Yep, this is how we came in." As Old Zhang led the way, the eight of us followed closely behind. Based on the distance we'd covered in the morning, we should have already emerged from there, but we had too much faith in our unit leader, not taking into account his poor eyesight.

We were surrounded by shrubs of uniform height with twigs of uniform thickness, and even somebody with good vision would have had a hard time distinguishing the path we came in by. We sensed Old Zhang was leading us in the wrong direction, and the farther we walked the deeper we entered the woods. It was then that we had made the crucial error of judgment in direction.

The farther we went, the denser the shrubs; the space between shrubs grew so small that we could no longer squeeze through. Clearly, this was an area that human beings had never penetrated. All we could do was stop and compose ourselves to try to ascertain our direction. But there were no reference points we could use. When we looked up we couldn't even see the sky, which was blocked by the thick cover of branches and leaves, nor could we see the sun or the moon, let alone any stars. All we were able to do was distinguish night and day by the light or darkness. For a long time we tried to figure out our direction, but we were really lost. "They say you can tell which direction is east by the side on which the branches are thicker and more abundant," said Old Xue. We looked. Damn it! That stupid stuff! The twigs on all sides grew upward uniformly. Our last ray of hope was gone.

Despondent, we limply sat down. To add to our troubles, it had grown dark. The chirping sound of all the different insects added to our hopeless and worried state. Zhang offered us forced encouragement. "The farther we go into untouched territory, the more confidence we need. Do you think that nine Bolsheviks can be defeated by a forest of shrubs? No way! Let's take out our rations and get some food in our stomachs and then have a good sleep. Tomorrow morning we'll find a way out, and leave this damned place forever!"

Hong Ling took his resentment out on our leader. "I saw all along, we never should have . . . "

Zhang laughed heartily, picking up his theme. "I admit it. I regarded myself as infallible. Comrade Hong Ling's original suggestion was correct . . . "

Hong Ling was too embarrassed to say any more.

I gnawed on the dried, crumbled bun in my hand. Without anything to drink, each mouthful tasted like grains of sand. I felt for the pellets of salt in my tooth powder bag and put one in my mouth, then another. My mouth finally began to feel a bit moistened. With that, I was able to eat some of the dry cornflour cakes. A bit of food in the stomach improves one's spirits tremendously. I felt carefree enough to tease Wang Lei. "I bet you never thought you'd have to suffer so much your first time in the revolution."

"I had some preparation. I imagined myself fighting side by side with my boyfriend, opening fire together against the devils from the east. But I never thought I'd end up a trapped rat in a place like this."

"Do you miss your guy?"

"Get away. What guy? We saw each other; I know he's alive, so I've stopped worrying. I don't miss him a bit!" she insisted, like a spoiled child.

Old Zhang interjected. "As soon as you stepped foot into the base area, you encountered this grim trial. I think you're really something—you should formally enter our ranks [the CCP]."

"How should we sleep tonight?" asked Wang Lei.

"Everyone find a spot and spread out your bedding," ordered Zhang. "You're a woman—according to Confucius's rules, you go away from us a bit and find a good level spot."

Within half an hour, we'd all found a place to sleep, and some were already snoring under their blankets. Suddenly we heard the howl of a wolf in the distance. Frightened, Wang Lei brought her bedding over with the men. "There's a wolf, I'm scared to be alone!" Old Zhang said softly, "Well, just sleep here with us." A minute later Zhang sat up and said to me, "We need to post a sentry to prevent a wolf attack."

"I'm not tired, I'll take the first watch."

"I'm not going to sleep tonight anyway, because of the wolf," said Wang Lei. "Let me keep watch—as soon as I see something I'll wake you."

Pulling out some tobacco, Zhang Chuanhe rolled a cigarette. "Let me take the lead. I'll do it for the first half of the night;

when I get tired, I'll wake you to take over.''

At this point, Wang Lei pulled out a shining flashlight from her securely fastened backpack and handed it to the unit leader. ''I brought it along. It's a good weapon against wolves.''

Zhang was pleased. ''How did you think to bring something like this? This is really useful. As soon as the wolf sees the bright light he won't dare come any closer.''

''My father bought it for me the night before I left home. My mother didn't know I was coming here; if she had, she definitely wouldn't have let me come. But my father supported me. He knew that Little Zhou—my boyfriend from high school—had come to the Communist base area. My father said, you should go there. I'm old and can't take part in the anti-Japanese resistance. But you young people should go. Go look for Little Zhou. It was my dad, behind my mother's back, who bought all this stuff. How thoughtful he was, even thinking to buy a flashlight. The only thing is, he shouldn't have bought the coffee pot. He thought in the countryside it was just as easy to brew coffee.''

''What does your father do?''

''He's a university professor. My mother's a teacher too; she teaches music.''

''You've got a good father,'' said Old Zhang. ''He's a true patriot.''

''My mother's not bad either. I really miss her. I imagine that after he sent me off my dad made up some story to fool her— poor Mama!'' Wang Lei's voice cracked. Zhang Chuanhe quickly comforted her. ''You've been running around all day, you must be worn out. Don't think about your family, get some sleep. I'll wake you to take over the watch.'' With a father's tenderness, he added, ''With me here, and this flashlight, the wolf won't come near; relax and get some sleep.''

''Old Zhang, wake me first. I'll take over the watch,'' I offered.

''Okay, all of you get some sleep. The ground here is as soft as a padded mattress. As soon as you lie down you'll be fast asleep.''

But I couldn't sleep. The woods, blown about by the night breeze, made a swishing sound like rain falling. A feeling of being trapped with no way out ate at my heart. And not ten steps away, an innocent and interesting young girl was lying, giving rise to all sorts of thoughts—of my own family, my wife, and of how the first time I left home I too tricked my mother and sneaked off.

I opened my eyes wide from the sudden bright beam of the flashlight and watched unit leader Zhang inspecting his troops. When the beam of light shined on Wang Lei, my eyes followed. She was sleeping peacefully, as if she hadn't experienced that day's rushing around and worries. Her dishevelled hair lay touching the dried branches and fallen leaves on the soft ground; her face seemed beautiful and tranquil, like a little girl in a cradle who had quickly entered dreamland. Her tightly pursed lips formed small dimples at the corners of her mouth. This was the first time I'd taken a good look at her, even though we'd been together for so many days. In the bright light I discovered her beauty.

The night was pitch dark and terrifying. Not only was the wolf howling, which was scary enough, but the quiet made my hearing particularly acute, enough to hear a soft "whooshing" sound a few feet away. What was it? A snake slithering nearby, or maybe some person creeping toward me in the darkness? On top of that was the grinding sound made by the branches as they blew in the wind; at times I felt that a huge army was battling above me. Despite all that, because I was totally exhausted, physically and mentally, I eventually dozed off. Only Old Zhang was left awake, forcing himself to keep his eyes open and watch in the darkness. We were like a flock of geese stopping on a sandy beach for the night, who sent out a few of their number to keep watch and sound the warning. In the ancient books they called this kind of goose a "slave goose"; Old Zhang was our "slave goose," protecting the flock.

IV

Eventually, the dark, frightening night was over. The next day the first person up saw Zhang Chuanhe sitting there, eyes open,

flashlight in hand. He had kept watch all night, not waking anyone to take over.

When Wang Lei woke up and saw how close she'd been lying
to the men, she blushed. "What should we do today?" she in-
quired.

Old Zhang laughed. "If your father had bought you a com-
pass, we'd be fine."

It was still gray and dark; the sky only provided some dim light,
and only a little at that. There wasn't a single watch among the nine
of us, so we didn't even know what time it was. "It's probably a
little past five o'clock," said Old Xue. "In a little while the sun will
rise and we should all observe carefully to see from which direction
the light comes earlier and stronger. I thought of it during the night;
it's a way that can get us out of here." Old Xue's full name was
Xue Zhengqing. He was a tailor in his thirties. He usually didn't say
much, but what he did say revealed an extraordinary intelligence
and rich experience. I think if he hadn't been a tailor, he could have
been a scientist—who knows?

We were encouraged by his suggestion and waited impatiently
for the sun to rise. Unfortunately, we waited a long, long time,
until the light of day was already quite bright. We could occa-
sionally see openings above, between the trees, but we couldn't
determine from which direction the light first came.

Old Xue frowned. "Damn it. Wouldn't you know, it's a
cloudy day today!"

"First fill your stomachs, then we'll decide what to do," said
Zhang Chuanhe.

Zhu Gang, a former elementary school teacher about thirty
years old, fumed, "This is called leaving the main road for a
dead end. Tired of living, we came here to die." He took his
empty ration bag and threw it at his feet. "And I'm out of rations." His words were clearly aimed at Zhang Chuanhe. Old
Zhang flushed but didn't respond.

Only then did Old Zhang realize that many of us were out of
food. Just four—myself, Old Zhang, Hong Ling, and Wang
Lei—still had enough rations for one or two meals. He grew

somber, but then optimistic and confident. "Let's distribute our food to those who've run out. We'll carry out another communist allocation! Politically, I'm still the leader, so I issue the following order: from now on, no more complaining or grumbling. The more dangerous it gets, the more united we need to be. I made an error in direction. When we've successfully emerged from this predicament, we'll have a meeting to criticize me."

I hadn't known Zhang very well. When he first became the leader of our group I thought he was a stubborn, opinionated fellow. He bore a heavy responsibility for our falling into this hopeless spot. But the way he kept watch all night and was now making such a firm decision made me admire him and realize he was a good leader.

The shortage of food constituted a greater threat to our unit than being lost. This breakfast finished off the rations the four of us had left, and we still weren't full. In the end we turned the bags inside out and ate every last crumb. The other severe threat was the lack of water. When your belly is empty you can still hold out for a while, but it's much harder to bear up when you can't get water. I thought back to that time in the Guomindang prison when we went on a hunger strike. We held out for five days, mainly because we had water to drink and some secret provisions. The reason I wasn't full after breakfast wasn't that there wasn't enough, but that there was no water with which to wash it down. The stuff was bone dry, impossible to swallow. Yesterday I'd mixed a few grams of salt to see if it would help, but for some strange reason this time when I added salt I got an unexpected result. It made all my food taste bitter, as if I'd eaten alum. I had to spit it all out.

Someone suggested we send out four people, one in each direction. Eventually one would find the way out. Whoever did would return by the same path and lead the rest of us out.

But this good idea was rejected. Old Zhang was really thorough. He felt that this plan was good in theory but in reality was extremely dangerous. Once somebody made it out, it would be very difficult for him to find his way back to this spot. There were no paths here—it was the same in all directions. As part of a group, a person can overcome any difficulty, but when he's alone, with no support and no one to rely on, he becomes weak and helpless, and his spirit may even collapse.

Old Xue then suggested, "We shouldn't send out troops in so many directions at once. I say we first send people in two directions, four people in all. The others stay here and wait. Those who go out should leave markings on the branches along their route so they won't get lost when they return." We all thought this was a good idea and began to think about how to leave the trail marks. We decided that the easiest and best method, and the clearest to spot, would be to take a Y-shaped branch and break one prong, leaving it hanging down.

Once again, Zhang Chuanhe volunteered to go out, but we refused to let him because he hadn't slept at all the night before. In the end, Old Xue and I took off in one direction and Hong Ling and somebody else set out the opposite way.

Old Xue and I went deep into the woods in search of a path. Every few steps we forcefully broke a branch to leave a mark. The density of the shrubs prevented us from going fast. It was impossible to calculate how far we'd gone in an hour. We were shouldering the heavy responsibility of being the "pathbreaking vanguard" and were hoping to be the first ones to emerge into the open. But we walked until we were dead tired, and the soles of my shoes had split from the uppers—damage easily done in those woods. We had to stop and rest.

We felt a powerful hunger overcome us, and we were terribly thirsty. We began to develop blisters on our lips, the corners of which were cracked. Old Xue helped me try to figure out a way to tie the soles back onto my shoes. He had been a tailor but never a cobbler, and although we played with it for a long time, there was no way since we didn't have any thread or string to tie it with, or any tools. But Old Xue was a real scientist. With a wink of his eye, he revealed a clever scheme. He broke off one of the branches and, starting from the tip, peeled off the bark all the way to the base. He fashioned two long, sturdy belts, and in the end I came away with a pair of sturdy shoes.

Old Xue was probably really hungry too, but he didn't say a word about it. "Should we keep pushing forward? Our stomachs are empty and we've come a long way and don't have the strength to go back. What do you say?"

To be frank, to try to make our way back to our unit would be exhausting. "If we go back now . . . we won't have accomplished our mission," I said with regret.

"Maybe the direction Hong Ling took was the right one," said Old Xue as he helped me up. We decided to return to camp.

Searching out our markers, we headed back to the group. I don't know why, but when we set out we'd been bold and spirited, and walked quickly. But going back we were like sick men, like fighting cocks who had been beaten; every step was an effort. How long did we walk before we returned to where Old Zhang and Wang Lei were waiting? Without a watch there was no way of knowing. But my guess is we walked a long, long time.

"No success?" Old Zhang asked anxiously.

Old Xue answered, "No."

Wang Lei came over to me with concern. "Your color doesn't look right."

"I know, it's from hunger. Hong Ling hasn't returned yet?"

"Not yet. I just hope they find a path out of here." She looked at my shoes. "Too bad we don't have a needle and thread—I'd like to sew those for you."

"It's okay, I can still wear them like this for a while."

I lay down on the ground listlessly. I thought back to our hunger strike that time. This experience was worse than that one. When you thought about it, this was only the first day without food; why was I so flustered, and why had the empty feeling already spread to my spine? I think it was because of the exertion of the day, which burned up a lot of energy, and also because there was no water to drink. Third, we hadn't had a full meal the two previous days, so the lining of my stomach was thin.

It was already dark by the time Hong Ling and his partner

returned. They hadn't found a way out either, but they had discovered an open area over a *mou** big. It looked as if people had once lived there, but the shrubs were so thick around it there was no way to tell which direction led out. They had intended to keep pushing ahead to look for a path, but they saw it was already getting dark and were afraid they wouldn't be able to see their branch markers, so they hurried back.

Zhang Chuanhe comforted them. "Don't worry about it. We'll find the way out tomorrow. The fact that everyone is back together is a victory."

The second dark night had arrived. Old Zhang arranged for two of us to keep watch, and in a tone of consolation said, "Our enemy now isn't the Japanese devils, but nature—wolves, darkness, and the endless woods."

"And hunger!" I added.

Before the words were out of my mouth, Wang Lei waved a hand in the air with something in it. "Comrades, I have sugar cubes and a package of coffee. I couldn't bear to throw them away. I'm turning them over to unit leader Zhang to distribute according to the principles of communism!"

This sudden and unexpected news filled us all with gratitude and warmth. Moved, Zhang Chuanhe accepted the packet. "You! I didn't know you were bursting with so much treasure!"

Hong Ling noted, "Coffee has a lot of vitamins and it's all right to eat it unbrewed. Comrade Wang Lei is a conscientious person—I suggest we give her a merit citation of the first rank."

"I don't want any merit citation. All I want is to get out."

Zhang counted the sugar cubes. "I want to suggest a distribution not based on simple egalitarianism. The owner who provided the sugar gets two shares, and the four comrades who went out today to search for the path also get two shares each—they worked harder than the rest of us. Do you agree?"

"We should give two shares to Wang Lei—no problem there," I responded. "As for two shares for those of us who went

---

*One-sixth of an acre.

out, I don't think it's necessary. It's good enough that we're not being punished for not accomplishing our mission. I suggest we give double shares to the people we send out tomorrow. By then our stomachs will really be empty, and it'll be harder for them to keep going. Let's not distribute the coffee yet—it'll be better to keep it in reserve.''

Everyone agreed, so that's what we did. This, despite Wang Lei's objections that since she hadn't borne the responsibility of going out that day, she had no right to an extra portion.

I received six lumps of sugar. I had begun to salivate in anticipation when we were still discussing how to distribute it. At the beginning I resolved to hold it in my mouth for a long time; how was I to know that as soon as it hit my mouth it would melt? After I swallowed it I rebuked myself for having no self-control, and a mouth that was too undisciplined. That evening I only ate five pieces; I had resolved to save one cube until the next day. Those five pieces made my empty stomach even hungrier, but I endured it and resisted eating the last cube. During the night, I was so hungry I couldn't sleep very well. Images of the hunger I had endured in prison eight years earlier kept going through my mind, with one difference: several scenes of having coffee kept appearing. Only when I opened my eyes to drive away this tempting but maddening vision did I realize that the coffee that Zhang Chuanhe was holding had become deeply ingrained in my subconscious. I hadn't thought about having coffee at all—the stuff had entered my mind on its own.

How I woke up on the morning of the third day, I've already forgotten. But there are two things that left an impression I'll never forget. The first was that when I went to get the last sugar cube I discovered to my horror that the paper wrapping was covered with ants. Frantic, I brushed them off. I was heartbroken to find that they had eaten a good part of the cube. Then I regretted that I had left the damned thing. Zhang Chuanhe found that the ants hadn't missed the coffee he was holding, either; the army of ants had already organized themselves in preparation for carrying off the whole thing. Zhang immediately took all the coffee and distributed it into nine portions—our breakfast for the day; no, our food for the whole day. I used the correct foreign method to finish off the coffee by mixing it with my remaining sugar. The only difference was that I didn't brew it with water; I just put it all in my mouth, letting it mix together. How can I describe it? It tasted like black sesame candy, or somewhat like eating bean paste cake. It was wonderful.

The second thing I'll never forget was that as soon as we finished our sweet breakfast, heaven did a bad thing to us—it began to rain. As the saying goes, "when the roof leaks you run into nonstop rain, when the ship is damaged you encounter head winds." We quickly wrapped our blankets and bedding into tight packs and tried to prevent the rain from soaking our belongings. At first Wang Lei put a reversible shirt made from water-repellent material over her head. But before long the rain grew heavier and heavier and her reversible shirt couldn't keep out the water. But Xue Zhengqing was optimistic. "Let's concentrate on receiving the water heaven is sending us—our thirst problem is over." With this reminder, everyone put his metal cup on the ground to catch the rain water. I saw Old Xue open his mouth wide to catch the water flowing from the leaves, and copied him. I was so busy swallowing the water that I forgot I was soaked from head to foot, forgot how cold I was getting. At that point, my greedy mouth wished it would rain even harder. While admiring Xue Zhengqing's resourcefulness, I enjoyed for the first time the satisfaction of "a sweet rainfall after a long drought." My thirst had made me feel like all my internal organs had contracted, like a machine that had burned up all its lubricating fluids—every movement was painful. But now that I had a few mouthfuls of water, it felt like every cell in my body relaxed and expanded. I could feel each spot the water traveled to inside my body. I saw everyone else craning their necks to catch the rain water, too. Clearly, they were as thirsty as I was.

Old Zhang decided that we should move, going first to the open area that Hong Ling had found. He believed that since people had once been there it couldn't be too far from an exit from the woods.

With Hong Ling in the lead, we moved out over the soaked ground. It was still raining, but since we were already drenched we didn't care. Our soaked trousers dragged against our legs, making it laborious to walk, and our backpacks had become heavier in the rain. We didn't bother wiping the rain off our faces. Wang Lei's hair, completely soaked, hung loosely on her shoulders. She looked like a goddess emerging from a river and was still cheerful in the midst of all this, humming the "guerrillas' song." Hong Ling picked up the tune, singing, " . . . In the woods dense and thick, each of us has turned into a drenched chick; high above on the mountain peak, where oh where our meal to seek?" His singing cheered us up considerably.

Old Zhang again took on the air of a leader. "Being a drenched rat doesn't matter, but don't let yourself become a beaten fighting cock." We laughed.

Talking and laughing the whole way, we eventually reached the open area. Without our noticing it, the rain had stopped, and for the first time we had a clear view of the sky. Although it was still dark and overcast, and black clouds chased one another through the sky, we felt a great sense of openness; the sky, which we hadn't been able to see for days, seemed especially clear and sharp. From our investigation of the place, we could see that people had once grown crops here and had burned firewood and cooked food; the blackened ashes still remained.

These signs of humanity were a great encouragement, and we decided to make camp here, then send out troops in two directions to find an exit. Old Zhang brought out the sugar he had put aside to reward the next day's scouts.

"Oh no!" he screamed. "It's all wet!"

Old Zhang was an extremely careful man. The thing he especially couldn't forgive himself for was that, having discovered the ants attacking his coffee, he hadn't thought of protecting the sugar. The expression "clever all one's life but stupid this one time" was probably apt.

Old Zhang stamped his feet. His bag of tobacco, too, was soaked. Even the matches were worthless. To a man with a heavy addiction to tobacco, this was an even bigger blow than the soaked sugar. We watched him greedily sniff the tobacco leaves, as if he were performing a departure ritual for a loved one, then, with firm resolve, throw away the whole bag.

As for the package of sugar drenched by the rain, Old Zhang began to lick it with his tongue, afraid that the sugar water would spill. Quickly reminded of "communist distribution," he hastily passed the sugar pack to Zhu Gang and Hong Ling. "It's really sweet—what a shame. Everyone have a taste." But no one was willing. Inside there, twenty-four cubes of sugar had shrunk drastically in size.

Wang Lei saw leader Zhang in this sorry plight, and gave him something she poured out of a glass jar. "I don't need this either, you all take it. It's just something to eat for fun."

Old Zhang took it in his outstretched hand and looked it over; it was chewing gum, wrapped in colored paper. He returned it to Wang Lei. "You were going to give this to Little Zhou. Keep it."

"I haven't got the vaguest idea what kind of mud hole Little Zhou is in now. He doesn't have the good fortune to eat this. The important thing now is to save ourselves, to keep up our strength and get out of this damned place. A piece of gum adds a little strength. You all eat it. Distribute it among yourselves, I don't want any."

You could see how much she missed him. Her lips said one thing, but her eyes said another: "So this is the kind of suffering Little Zhou is going through in the base area. Like him, I'm in a mud hole now too!"

We distributed Wang Lei's last bit of private property. We were now old friends, and with the gum in our mouths we didn't say a word of thanks. Instead, we teased her. "What right do we have to eat your gum? Only Little Zhou has the right. I'd really like to become him, to enjoy this little bit of sweetness."

Hong Ling interrupted. "Twice today we received life-saving sweets. The credit should go to Little Zhou. If he weren't in the base area, and if it weren't for Wang Lei's deep love and great kindness, we'd really have gone hungry. We wouldn't have been able to enjoy the sweet taste of coffee.''

Wang Lei blushed and replied, a bit angrily. ''All right, all right. If I knew how you all gossiped, I wouldn't have given you these things! I'll tell you, my dear old friends: I used to think that love was the noblest and purest emotion. Now I believe that revolutionary friendship is just as noble and pure.''

VI

Our scouts still hadn't returned; the sugar and gum had long since been digested. Although the rain had stopped, the leaves were still wet and sprinkled us when the wind blew.

Leaning against his soaked backpack, Hong Ling had fallen asleep. We had been living like prehistoric beings these three days, and he was clearly thinner. His clothes were still wet through. You couldn't help but feel sorry for him. It made me sad to realize that if I looked in a mirror I'd see my condition wasn't any better than his. I looked again at Old Zhang and Old Xue. They were in an equally sorry state. In his heart, Old Zhang was even more anxious, but he maintained a calm and unperturbed exterior, never forgetting to keep up the morale of the troops.

A gray grasshopper jumped onto Hong Ling's sleeping head and stopped there for a rest. But it didn't wake him. I had to catch the thing quickly to keep it from disturbing Hong Ling's sleep—this, at least, was something within my power to do. With a quick movement I caught the grasshopper in my hand without waking Hong.

''Did you catch it?'' asked Old Xue, as I was about to kill it.

''Yep, I got him.''

''You can eat grasshoppers—they're nourishing. In Shandong one year we had a plague of locusts, and we cooked them as regular food.''

I gave the grasshopper to Old Zhang. ''I understand you can eat it if you cook it. But with everything wet, how can we cook it?''

"You can eat them raw. There's no such thing as a hopeless situation for man." Then he pinched off the grasshopper's head. "Watch me eat it." As if it were a deep-fried shrimp, he popped the raw thing into his mouth and swallowed it with apparent relish. Tempted by his example and driven by unrelenting hunger, I tried to catch more grasshoppers in the brush. Old Xue and the others joined me. Later Hong Ling woke up and he too participated, becoming an active member of our grasshopper-catching group. Only Wang Lei, who was scared of grasshoppers and certainly wouldn't eat them, observed from the sidelines.

I wasn't too successful. I only caught two. I wouldn't dare chew the first one, so swallowed it whole. Only with the second did I get any of the taste, and I can tell you that although it didn't taste as good as deep-fried shrimp, it wasn't bad. Hong Ling said the nourishment in one grasshopper was equivalent to one cube of sugar or five pieces of gum.

With the ground still wet from the recent rain it was hard to catch the things. I didn't catch any more for a long time, but I didn't give up. I accidentally came upon several green worms that looked like silkworms, climbing up the branches of the shrubs. They were a bit longer than a silkworm when it's about to spin its cocoon—actually, they were the larvae of moths or butterflies. I caught one and, holding it in the palm of my hand, showed it to Old Xue, who said, "When we were small we used to catch 'beanworms' in the fields, the same size as these. We used sorghum stalks to light a fire to cook them, and they were quite good. This isn't a 'beanworm,' but it's from the same family. I think you can eat it. There's no such thing as a hopeless situation for man." He popped the worm into his mouth with no hesitation and ate it with pleasure.

Then we began to catch the green larvae. Hong Ling caught quite a few, but for some reason he didn't eat a single one. The nerve he'd shown when he ate the grasshopper was gone, and he gave his worms to me. I was stronger than he and had no inhibitions—I could eat anything at that point. During the course of the day I tasted two kinds of worms. The green larvae were better than the grasshoppers and tasted kind of like a raw egg. As for a live larva, if you weren't on the verge of starvation, you wouldn't be able to put it in your mouth without getting sick.

Wang Lei was on the side, laughing at us. "What a group of barbarians you've become. Never mind eating them—just watching you stick one green worm after another into your mouths is making me sick."

"When you're hungry enough to die, you'll be able to swallow them too," I replied. "During famines in the countryside, people in a lot of places eat 'Guanyin dirt'* and rats; they can do it because they're so hungry they have no choice."

"That's for sure," echoed Old Xue. "In 1932 I ate 'Guanyin dirt' and the bark of trees; a grasshopper was considered a piece of meat."

Old Zhang reasoned, "This is good stuff, locally grown. If you can't eat it, look at it as medicine, or a kind of tonic, and you'll be able to get it down."

"Right, it's a good tonic," agreed Hong Ling.

"How come *you* can't eat the larvae? I think four of them is worth one egg," I teased him.

"I can't explain why. I've never been able to stand worms—like a Muslim who doesn't eat pork." This reminded me of the hunger strike in prison, and a conversation with Zhang Yunqing.

Zhang Chuanhe issued a sudden order. "We have four comrades who haven't returned yet. It's our responsibility to prepare food for them."

So we took the empty jar from Wang Lei's gum and threw the green larvae inside; this would be their food.

Before dark the two pairs of scouts returned. One pair had done the "devil's circle" not very far away. The "devil's circle" means losing your way in the dark and going in circles, thinking you're going very far when in fact you're just circling the same

---

*Guanyin is a bodhisattva of compassion. "Guanyin dirt" is a white clay eaten by famine victims in some parts of old China.

area. Dizzy from hunger or for some other reason, these two had been circling all this time and walked themselves into a state of exhaustion. The other pair was also unsuccessful. One of them was weak and fainted en route, and his partner Zhu Gang had to half carry him back. Zhu Gang let out a long sigh upon his return. "We can't get out." Then he collapsed to the ground. Five or six of us rushed over to help him up. His teeth were clenched, his eyes closed, and his face white. Hong Ling pressed his ear to Zhu's chest. "He's fainted, probably because of hunger and exhaustion. His heart is still beating, though slowly. He won't die." Xue Zhengqing took off his underclothes, by now dry, removed Zhu's wet ones, and put his own on Zhu. Then he held him in his arms. The ground was so wet there wasn't a dry spot to lie on. Zhu Gang finally regained consciousness and asked, weakly, "Will we be able to get out?"

Zhang Chuanhe gently rubbed Zhu's head. "Don't worry, we'll find a way out." I could tell he was just saying this to comfort him and that he really didn't have any confidence. His quivering tone did not conceal his despair and fear. He opened the jar and pulled out a live larva. He twisted off the head and said to Zhu Gang, "Eat something, you must be starving." He put the larva into Zhu's mouth. "Try this. It's medicine that can restore your energy." He winked at the rest of us.

Zhu Gang chewed it. "Where did this come from? From Wang Lei again?"

Zhang Chuanhe lied, smoothly. "It's dried beef, contributed by Wang Lei." Old Zhang was a straight guy who couldn't lie convincingly. Zhu Gang could tell. "This isn't dried beef." Old Zhang was preparing to feed him another one, but Zhu closed his mouth and opened his eyes. "I'll eat it myself." Old Zhang insisted, "Let me feed you," sliding another one into his mouth.

Zhu had quickly figured out that it wasn't dried beef, but Old Zhang doggedly kept up the deception, saying, "This is dried beef from Japan." Wang Lei, standing on the side, could barely keep from laughing.

Zhu Gang gradually regained some strength from the "dried Japanese beef."

I had eaten a lot of the "dried beef" myself, so I was in very good spirits. "Japanese dried beef has two special features: one is that you get the materials locally, the other is you catch it and eat it—it's fast and convenient."

So there we were in the woods catching worms, like barbarians in a primitive commune, storing away the surplus from the hunt in Wang Lei's glass jar. The only difference was the glass jar—that was something primitive man didn't have.

Near the base of the branches I discovered a new kind of creature. It was like the green larvae, with a soft body and no legs, and a bright crystal-like substance on it. I had seen these as a small child. I caught one and showed it to Old Xue, who said, "You can't eat this. It's a house centipede. Little kids call it a snot bag. Wherever it goes, it leaves a shiny trail."

"If we became house centipedes and left a shiny trail wherever we went, we wouldn't get lost."

It gradually grew dark. Looking up, you couldn't see a single star. Old Xue was frustrated. "If there were just some stars in the sky, we would have a way to fix the directions."

"We're going to be trapped here until we die," said Zhu Gang.

"Logically, one of the two paths we took today should have led out. It wasn't that they couldn't find the way out; they just didn't have the strength to get there."

Zhang Chuanhe was concerned about Wang Lei. "We all got some dried beef, but you didn't eat anything. How will you survive? If I'd known, I would have left more of the sugar for you."

She smiled bitterly. "I never encountered hunger growing up, but I sure have now. I can make it, maybe because of that extra piece of sugar you gave me."

"Be brave and eat a little of this local specialty. Cantonese eat grown worms and rats—what are you afraid of?"

Wang Lei firmly refused.

Zhang Chuanhe announced, "Tomorrow I'll go with Xue Zhengqing to look for a way out. I don't believe we can't get out of here."

"In that case, eat the dried beef so you'll have strength," I suggested.

Within ten minutes, several in the group had already climbed into their bedrolls. Zhang had fallen asleep propped against some tree trunks. No one bothered keeping watch anymore, and the sound of wolves didn't frighten us.

We were each tormented by hunger and were wet and cold. We curled up into tight circles like shrimp. No one would admit that death was following us through the woods. Despite using all our wits and energy, we still couldn't break out of this tight encirclement.

This was the lowest night of my life, the hardest to take. It was bad enough that my stomach was empty and rumbling; the biggest threat was that there was no way out. These woods were like the mazes described in ancient novels: once you went in, forget about getting out. After two days of scrambling and searching, we were still without a clue. And with the passing of each hour, we used up a bit more of our strength.

VII

It was not yet fully light. Steamy vapor had begun to rise in the woods and covered the dense growth with a layer of white dust. It was as quiet as a graveyard—I'd been awakened by the early morning cold of autumn. As soon as I woke up my head felt heavy and there was a bitter taste in my mouth. I wanted to spit it out, but I was parched and nothing came out. I looked around for some "dried beef" for breakfast but came up empty. What I did discover, to my surprise, was dew on the leaves, which I licked and licked, thinking how resourceful I was. After I'd consumed a large amount, a strange pheonomenon occurred: the bitter taste in my mouth dissipated and the blisters on my lips shrank. I quickly woke up my companions nearby and told them to drink the dew.

It was then that I spotted a wolf approaching us, not far away. The hair on my body stood on end, and I shouted, "It's a wolf!" At least I had enough courage to wake Wang Lei and Hong Ling, who, because they hadn't eaten the "beef," were visibly tired and weak. Zhang Chuanhe turned pale and his eyes bulged. He motioned for us to go deeper into the woods. "It won't be hard to take care of one wolf with this many people," he comforted us.

Zhu Gang was already very weak and hardly able to move at all. But when he heard me shout he jumped three or four feet and headed into the woods.

Wang Lei entered the brush and knelt on the ground, her eyes fixed on the wolf across the way. "If he'd come during the night it would have been a disaster. He would have had a ready-made meal."

"Don't make any noise," cautioned Xue Zhengqing. "Everyone watch him."

The wolf's eyes glowed, and he kept sniffing the ground. He had definitely picked up the human scent and had followed it step by step to this open area. Our backpacks were all on the ground. The wolf sniffed Old Zhang's empty water bottle and Wang Lei's glass jar, then licked Hong Ling's satchel.

The nine of us were silent, holding our breath as we watched the wolf. Each of us was trying to guess which one he would leap toward.

"Look. It's not a wolf, it's a dog!" said Xue Zhengqing. The animal seemed to understand him and raised its head and looked over at us.

"The main difference is the tail," said Old Zhang. "It doesn't look like a wolf's. His tail curls up; a wolf's tail droops."

"Let's try to catch him and have him guide us out of here," suggested Old Xue.

We thought this would be dangerous; who was going to catch him? Where would a dog come from in these deep woods? Maybe it *was* a wolf.

What happened next takes a long time to tell, but it occurred in an instant. Old Xue whispered to me, "Give me the two straps from your shoes, quickly!'' I untied them and threw them over. The next thing I knew, Old Xue was walking into the open. I guess he changed his plan, because he didn't use my shoe straps but detached the ration bag from his backpack and threw it toward the animal. The sack had a fragrance that attracted the dog. It came over and sniffed at it, then began to lick it. We breathed an immense sigh of relief. As we made the mental transition from wolf to dog, Old Xue, holding one end of the sack, deftly moved around behind the dog, which was still trying to find something to eat in it. Old Xue grabbed the other side of the sack and pulled it under the dog's stomach. It wanted to turn around and bite him, but Old Xue had already bound the sack up with a knot, and the dog was trapped. What a display of courage and decisiveness! I had to admire Old Xue for his skill and dexterity.

Xue Zhengqing had become a victorious general. ''It's a dog. Definitely a dog. Let's all get moving. We'll follow him.''

We felt our spirits rise. We bent over to pick up our things and, with Old Zhang ahead and Old Xue holding the pack, followed the dog. Since the now discarded bark straps had been the only thing keeping my shoes together, before too long they fell apart and I had to go barefoot. Moving swiftly to keep up with the group, I developed blood blisters. But I didn't feel any pain— I kept going forward, following that dog with everything I had. Even stranger, my stomach didn't feel empty. I just had a hard time catching my breath.

Xue Zhengqing held one end of the pack and allowed the dog to run ahead of him. The dog would go very quickly, then stop to take a leak, then move forward again with no hesitation. It was magic. We didn't travel far before coming to the end of the woods. Seeing the endless azure blue sky above was like seeing our own lives, our futures, before us. We yelled wildly, ''Hallelujah! We made it! We're saved!''

Before us was a great plain, exactly the opposite of the dense growth that had encircled us. Far off in the distance, white clouds rose gently from the plain. It felt like we'd been separated from this plain for a long time. I greedily sucked in the damp, fresh air.

"How about that? I've made it back again!"

We were like primitive men from the Stone Age who'd just emerged from a primeval forest. Our clothes had been ripped and torn by the branches; some had been torn into strips. I didn't even have any shoes. Only after we emerged from the woods did the sores on my feet begin to ache.

Wang Lei pulled the dog over to her and rubbed his head affectionately. "How can we thank you? You're our savior." She untied the pack from around him but he didn't move away. He licked the back of Wang Lei's hand. Then it dawned on her. "I recognize him. He's from the home of those two brothers."

Zhang Chuanhe rubbed the dog's soft pelt, as if greeting a dog he knew well. "I can't tell, but the color of his fur sure is the same."

In this moment of excitement and happiness, several of us, myself included, lay down limply on the ground, our feet like wood, unable to move another step. The bright light of the open space seemed to have an effect on us. We hadn't noticed our empty stomachs before, but now we were unbearably hungry. It felt like I'd been cut off at the waist; it was even worse than the feeling I had on the last day of our five-day hunger strike years back.

In that deliberately stern tone of his, Zhang Chuanhe commanded, "Get up right away and keep following this great dog. Don't relax now, gather your strength, and we'll follow him to a village where we can get something to eat!" Then he dropped his commander's tone. "Those who want to live, who want to eat, hurry up and follow me."

To my surprise, Old Xue, lying weakly on the ground, pounded the crook of his knee with his fist. He was the first to stand. Gritting his teeth to support his unsteady body, he walked up to Zhang and grabbed his backpack. "Let me carry it!"

Zhang loosened Xue's hand from the pack. "I'll carry it—you're not well. Take care of the dog; we still need him to lead us."

I, too, summoned my energy to bring myself to a standing position. Zhang's rallying power came from his own command, "those who want to eat, hurry up and follow me." Even if it meant risking my life, I had to go with him. When you know you're down and at the end of your rope, as soon as there's a ray of hope, even if you're on the verge of death you can suddenly become a dragon or tiger, with head high, prepared to make a heroic effort.

Inspired by unit leader Zhang, I grabbed Wang Lei's knapsack, thinking, she's a woman just come from the big city to the base. She's undergone so much with us. She didn't even have the energy to carry her pack anymore, and she hadn't eaten anything for several days. She was obviously drained from the heavy rain and sleepless nights. She didn't bother to comb her dishevelled hair, now dried, but let it hang down to her shoulders. She wouldn't let me carry her pack, but I grabbed it from her anyway. If she hadn't been a woman, I would have picked her up off the ground. Eventually, she managed to get herself up and joined the group.

The nine of us formed an orderly line. Following closely behind the dog, we limped our way toward the plain. I walked next to Wang Lei and tried my best to say encouraging things to keep her spirits up. "What are you thinking now?" I asked.

"I'm thinking about having a nice meal; even eating a few sweet potatoes would be okay."

"What else?"

"I think," and she paused a moment, "I'll write a long letter to my mother."

"That night we couldn't make our way out of here I thought to myself, if we don't get out tomorrow, we'll die in here."

"I thought the same thing," she responded.

The dog broke out into a run; panting and gasping, we tried to keep up. He was making a bee-line for the houses of the two brothers up ahead in the distance. No question about it now, this life-saving dog was indeed an old friend. And so the nine of us rallied our last bit of energy and headed for the familiar house. Gradually, even the gourd vines of the roof became clearly visible. Just at this point, Zhu Gang collapsed to the ground. Like the day before, his eyes closed, his lips turned white, and there were beads of sweat on his forehead. Zhang Chuanhe rubbed Zhu's upper lip with his finger, shouting, "Zhu Gang! Zhu Gang!" Hong Ling knelt on the ground to listen to his heart. "His heartbeat is very weak." The dog, seeming to understand, stopped and came back to Zhu Gang's side, sniffing at his hands and feet.

Xue Zhengqing said, "You all hurry to the farmhouse and speak with the owner. Ask him to bring some gruel or some rice broth. I'll stay here with him."

We headed for the tiny settlement as quickly as we could. When the owner saw us coming, he gladly put on the rice gruel.

When we told him that one of our comrades had fallen nearby and needed food, he quickly picked up a gourd and scooped out some *hutu* [a kind of gruel Shandong people make from sorghum and cornflour] from a wooden bucket and headed out. Zhang Chuanhe pointed the way. That amazing yellow dog ran up to his owner, took a few steps forward, stopped, and looked back as if to say, "I know, follow me."

The old man told Zhang Chuanhe to remain, that he'd go himself. The dog would lead him. Zhang stayed behind but told the old man, "There's also Comrade Xue—let him eat a little *hutu* too, otherwise he'll never have the strength to make it back."

About an hour later, Xue Zhengqing, supporting Zhu Gang, returned. Old Zhang embraced Zhu Gang and said to the farmer, "We owe it all to you. If it weren't for you we'd have died—there was nothing we could do. Now we're completely victorious!"

The rice gruel was ready. I didn't care how hot it was. Even though it burned the roof of my mouth, I greedily and happily swallowed that golden-colored gruel.

After eating, I felt like a new man. I explained to the farmer at length and with great praise how his dog had saved our lives.

The farmer gave the dog two pieces of sweet potato as a reward. "He's really smart. Sometimes he runs into the woods and doesn't come back for a day or two. There are pheasant in there, and one morning he came out with one in his mouth. So he knows the way out pretty well."

He also talked about the clearing in the woods, which the brothers had made their first year here. They'd been afraid that a landlord would come take away any land that was already cleared, so they used a patch in the woods, not visible. They planted maize on it, but all the nutrients in the soil must have been consumed by the thorn bushes, because they never even recovered their seeds. Besides, the plot was too hard to reach, so the next year they abandoned it.

We had made it through a great disaster, and spent a couple of days resting with the two brothers. Compared to the Stone Age existence of a few days before, eating rice gruel in the old farmer's house was like being in heaven.

Two days later we headed off in the direction of Boxing and Huimin—that was where our troops normally camped. After walking twenty miles we ran into some comrades from the Eighth Route Army. We learned from them that the Japanese mop-up campaign had reached Boxing but had met a ferocious counterattack from our side. The Japanese had retreated helter skelter, and there wasn't a single one left in the old base area. We also found out that the scattered units of the rear service forces had been ordered to go to the Lijinwa *area*, not to the Lijinwa woods. It turned out that we had been careless and had misunderstood. When we realized the source of our mistake, none of us wanted to go into the question of individual responsibility. It was our fate—if you're doomed, you're doomed. We looked at each other with smiles on our faces and let it pass.

Only Wang Lei still clung to her hope of catching a Japanese soldier. "If they'd sent me to the real army at the beginning, maybe I could've caught one of those devils."

"This time I guarantee you'll get to see some Japanese soldiers," promised Xue Zhengqing.

"I suffered so much with all of you and never got to see a single one. What a waste . . . where do we go? Do I need to bring a gun?"

"I'll take you to see some Japanese POWs. You don't need a gun."

"I'm not interested in seeing POWs. I'd been planning to write to my mother to tell her I've gone to the front to fight the devils. What do I write her now?"

Hong Ling teased her. "Your first task now isn't to go see Japanese POWs or to write your mother—it's to find Little Zhou."

"You rat!" screamed Wang Lei, chasing after Hong. "Your mouth is faster than my own thoughts. Grab him, the Japanese devil, the mischievous rat!"

Time passes quickly. Thirty years later when I went looking for the woods they were gone. In their place were the steel frames of oil wells standing on a vast plain. The Shengli Oil Field is set right on the spot of the great woods.

Hunger Trilogy

Part 3

I

IN THE SUMMER of 1966 I suddenly became a "cow." Under the slogan "away with all cow-devils and snake-spirits," I was put in the "cowshed" together with other cadres and intellectuals.

All work was at a standstill. The whole day was spent putting up big-character posters, singing quotations from Chairman Mao, holding struggle sessions, and beating the gong and drum in taking "glad tidings" to the Municipal Revolutionary Committee. Partaking in any other activities was considered working for revisionism. While locked up in the "cowshed" another "cow-devil" and I were allowed to carry buckets of glue to paste up big-character posters and slogans in the streets. At that time the walls lining Shanghai's streets and alleyways were covered with big-character posters. The amount of ink, paper, and glue consumed for this purpose far outweighed all the steel being produced in the factories at the time.

What did the big-character posters say? We never bothered to look. It was just our job to paste them up. On this particular day we had just arrived at the Cathay Theater on Huaihai Road, when suddenly we saw a surging mass of people clustered around several slow-moving trucks. In each truck stood a row of criminals with large boards hanging across their chests revealing their names and reactionary titles. Standing behind each criminal was a youth wearing a Red Guard armband. Especially striking were two trolley company repair vehicles. These red trucks had platforms that could be elevated seven feet into the air to repair cables. Looking up I saw an old man with white hair standing on one of the platforms. The bystanders looked up at him, shouting, "Look! It's Cao Diqiu! And that's his stinking wife behind him!" The truck was deliberately driven slowly; I continued to gaze up at the old man with white hair. Shifting position, I could make out the name on his placard—"Big Traitor Cao Diqiu."* My heart constricted. Tearfully, I looked back up at Cao Diqiu with his hands tied behind his back and wept to myself, "Old Zhang! How did you get up there?"

The truck drove slowly down Central Huaihai Road, as if rolling straight across my chest.

In a flash I recalled the Old Zhang I'd known in the 1930s, the nutrition expert incarcerated in the pigeon cage at Caohejing. After he got out of prison, using his real name, Cao Diqiu, he went to the New Fourth Army area and served as administrative head of Yanfu, as party secretary of Northern Jiangsu District, and in other top posts. How could a leading cadre of the municipal Party Committee who had withstood the tests of imprisonment and war turn into a traitor just like that? And how could such people be treated like criminals and paraded through the streets for the edification of the masses?

Platform trucks are used to repair trolley cables; who could have thought up the idea of using them to parade the municipal party secretary and mayor around in dunce caps? This was the bitterest joke on earth, a joke perpetrated by the entire dictatorship, indeed, a madness devoid of all reason enveloping every single person in the country.

My fellow inmates in the "cowshed" heard that every leader on the Shanghai Municipal Committee except Zhang Chunqiao had had placards hung around his neck and been marched through the streets, and that some had even been placed on the platform of the repair truck. We grew restless. Everyone ner-

---

*Cao Diqiu was secretary of the Secretariat of the Shanghai Municipal CCP Committee and mayor of Shanghai. He eventually died on March 29, 1976, at the age of sixty-seven. a victim of prolonged persecution by the "Gang of Four."

vously prepared to be marched out on the street and hung with boards for the masses to see. We were antsy even at meals during those few days, sure that at any moment the order would sound for us to be put into trucks and paraded through the streets. Even at night we dreamed of being marched around: in one dream it was me standing on the platform of the truck, as if watching the Greet the Spirits Celebration as a child.* Surrounding me were curling white clouds; I was enveloped in mist. When I awoke I was covered in cold sweat. I figured I probably wasn't qualified to stand on the truck. And if I were hung with a placard along with everyone else, I had a way to hide my face—my plan was to look as if I were very ashamed by bending down from the waist and lowering my head. There was a writer named Fu who planned to die in order to avoid this march through the streets. He once whispered to me, "I don't have the courage to stand on that truck, but I do have the courage to die." The atmosphere in the "cowshed" was tense, terrifying. The great disaster we had foreseen was about to arrive.

One day passed, two days passed. We waited, but in the end it never happened and we rejoiced inwardly. It was only afterward that we found out our unit was too small to have access to trucks. The rebels went everywhere trying to borrow one, but trucks were in particular demand at that time. Other units were busy parading their own cow-devils and snake-spirits through the streets, so our unit was unable to locate a truck. By the time they got their hands on one, the higher-ups came out with the order forbidding any more marching through the streets. We had escaped this calamity by a fluke, and everyone breathed a sigh of relief, especially Fu. I took the opportunity to chide him a bit: "How worthless it would have been to kill yourself! What if you had really died? In hell you would have found out we weren't marched out after all. You'd regret your act, feel ashamed, and

---

*The Greet the Spirits Celebration (*yingshen saihui*) is a generic term for a religious folk event. The spirits and gods honored differ from place to place and festival to festival, but the celebration generally includes a parade or a race of some sort.

hate yourself. So no matter what, don't commit suicide, okay?'' Looking at me like a benefactor who had saved his life, he nodded silently.

Following this episode came the so-called investigators. First came one group, the rebel faction from Guangxi Province, who wanted me to provide information relating to Xu Yushu's stay in prison. I told them the truth, but they weren't interested. They didn't even take notes. Rather, one of them asked me over and over whether or not Xu had recanted or turned traitor. I said he had not. They were highly disappointed; they wanted me to think it over really carefully. Then the tension increased and finally I said, ''I don't know. If you think there was something up with him while he was under arrest, go ask somebody else!''

The following day another group came to see me. This time they were young people calling themselves the Municipal Party Committee Rebel Faction. They wanted me to disclose how Cao Diqiu had crawled out of the enemy's dog hole [escaped from prison]. ''I don't know about that,'' I answered. ''I only know that in prison he proved himself a Bolshevik; he was staunch and optimistic.''

''No. He was a traitor, a big traitor.''

''You weren't in prison with him. How would you know?''

''We already know his record well, and Jiang Qing said he was a big traitor.''

''Since Comrade Jiang Qing knows he was a terrible traitor, go ask her about it! Why ask me?''

''No, we still need proof,'' one of the youths from the Municipal Party Committee Rebel Faction said rudely.

''Cao Diqiu's standing on the truck that day already decided his case. What more proof do you want?''

My responses disappointed them. They gave me a vicious look just as they were about to leave, and one of the leaders snapped, ''You're covering up for him; you're a shit, too.''

From then on the investigators came one after another, inquiring about one person or trying to prove something about another. Each day several people came to see me. Soon I caught on to the temperament of the "rebels." If you said so-and-so behaved well, they were not interested, but if you portrayed Communist Party cadres as traitors and spies they were all smiles, as if they had hit the jackpot. So after spending hundreds of millions of state dollars and mobilizing hundreds of thousands of people in this nationwide investigation, the material dug up amounted to nothing but a pile of trash (perhaps some of the material was factual, but this was rare in the extreme). The practical results were even worse than the creation of "waste paper," for such painstaking efforts under the guise of "investigation" were used to fabricate slander as false evidence against fine people.

During the era when framing people was the order of the day, the rebels finally announced that I would be locked up in isolation in my office. At that time every work unit had constructed a holding room and tribunal. Knowing that I would not escape this calamity, I had mentally prepared myself for it early on.

After locking me up they wanted me to sign a false dossier prepared by the rebel faction's special investigation group. Not signing it would constitute "serious resistance," and they would have a few people wear me down or punish me viciously to force me to confess I was a traitor. When I looked over the "false dossier" I was both furious and amused. The material cited as evidence was nothing more than a big-character poster signed by two people. What's more, while I had been facing hunger in a Guomindang prison, one of them hadn't even been born yet, and the other was still in diapers! When I refused to sign this deceptive and false document, the "Special Investigation Group" read from *Chairman Mao's Quotations* and threatened, "If you continue to be obstinate, this will turn into a contradiction between us and the enemy."*

---

*In "On the Correct Handling of Contradictions Among the People," written in 1957, Mao Zedong delineated his thesis of "contradictions between ourselves and the enemy" as "antagonistic contradictions" and those "within the ranks of the people" as "nonantagonistic." In the first case, "counterrevolutionaries" are defined as "the enemy," thus the author was put in the enemy camp.

As in any juggling act, the concepts of internal contradictions among the people and those between us and the enemy can be tossed back and forth at will. This sounded pretty funny to me. "I am what I am," I thought to myself. "Nobody can tack on anything to what happened several decades ago, nor can anyone detract from it."

So what if it did become a contradiction between us and the enemy? Before long they handcuffed me and escorted me to the detention quarters of the Public Security Organ.* They called this "being elevated a rank." This term originally had a good connotation, but here everything was turned topsy-turvy, and "being elevated a rank" signified sinking to the lowest depths of hell.

The guard led me into an interrogation room. Wearing shiny handcuffs, I walked down a long hall and came to a dim, stuffy room. At once, I recalled the time forty-three years ago when I was arrested by the Guomindang and interrogated and tortured in this very place by a KMT spy from the Special Municipal Party Branch. The room had one heavy and crude square bench, on both sides of which were attached leather restraining straps. This concrete proof convinced me that I had been here before. The only features that distinguished the two time periods were the framed picture of Chairman Mao and the couplets hanging on either side: "Leniency to those who confess!" and "Severity to those who resist!"

The questioning began. I realized they were totally uninterested in the crime of the accused or whether or not there were grounds for the accusation. The basis of their interrogation was

---

*The Public Security Organ (Gongjianfa) was a Cultural Revolution entity composed of three previously separate organs—the Public Security Bureau (Gonganju), Procuracy (Jianchayuan), and Court of Justice (Fayuan). During the Cultural Revolution, these three organs were combined and given the sole task of incarcerating "criminals," their earlier functions and relationship of checks and balances having been eliminated. For a discussion of these organs and their changing roles, see Victor H. Li, "The Public Security Bureau and Political-Legal Work in Huiyang, 1952–64," in *The City in Communist China*, ed. John Wilson Lewis (Stanford: Stanford University Press, 1971), especially pp. 53, 71, 73.

nothing more than the order from above that so-and-so should be overthrown. When the Guomindang had interrogated Communist Party members they were after only true statements, yet when counterfeit Communist Party members interrogated real Communist Party members, they didn't want the truth; they were only after lies.

To each question I responded to the effect that "I seem to have been here before."

The interrogator looked at me coldly. "You are a recidivist. No wonder you refuse to mend your ways despite repeated admonitions."

"Because of my beliefs I was arrested some forty years ago and a Guomindang spy actually interrogated me in this very room." I was unable to suppress my wrath.

The interrogator's face turned white. "This proves that you were an old revolutionary. I've seen lots of old revolutionaries turn into old counterrevolutionaries. Even here you want to talk smart. Okay. I could have taken your handcuffs off, but because you're so disruptive, I couldn't possibly be lenient with you."

Thus my first interrogation hurriedly concluded. I walked out of the small room I had once been in long ago; the guard led me to a prison lined with two rows of cells and pushed me through one of the black iron doors. The room through the iron door measured roughly fifteen or sixteen square meters. Sixteen criminals already were incarcerated in its oppressive darkness. Overcrowding was the most hazardous aspect of all the prisons during the "Great Cultural Revolution." Because of my handcuffs and white hair, the prisoners took me for a very serious offender. No one spoke for a long time, sizing me up with suspicious and probing eyes.

II

I couldn't help but compare the cell to the one I had occupied forty years earlier. It was quite different. The room of forty years ago had no window in the back; inmates used a commode to relieve themselves, so the air was foul and stifling. But this cell had four windows in the back. The toilet was a hole opening through to the outside made at a 90-degree angle in the back corner with a concrete ditch for squatting. Although this was a far cry from a flush toilet, it was much more "modern." There was one more striking difference: the time I was shut up in that dark prison, I was the youngest one there. Now, with my white hair, I was the oldest. Most of the sixteen others with me were under thirty, with the exception of a fellow named Cai, who was forty-six at the time. I forget the rest of his name, but I remember his number—1207.

Wang Weiguo was the head of Shanghai's Public Security Organ at the time. He had a whole bunch of theories about prisoner treatment. Once he said that if you let counterrevolutionaries eat their fill, their rations would be the same as a regular person's, so many citizens would be happy to be counterrevolutionaries. And then there were his two slogans on treating prisoners: "No benevolent policies for counterrevolutionaries." "Mercy toward the enemy is cruelty to your comrades." This set of theories transformed most of the obedient prison guards into inhumane "hachet men" who tormented the prisoners mentally and physically. It was also under the influence of Wang Weiguo's "revolutionary spirit" that prisoners' grain rations were reduced to below the minimal standard, and relatives were forbidden to bring in any food. We ate only two meals a day. The containers holding our food were almost identical in size and shape to the ones forty years ago. But they held less food than what the Guomindang had given political prisoners, and the pickled vegetables were not as good as those in the Guomindang jail.

The inmates had not yet lost their sense of humor; they called the food here "Sichuanese cooking" because Shanghainese pronounce the word for "water" (*shui*) just like the "Si" in Sichuan. *Shuichuancai* (water-boiled vegetables) referred to the vegetable scraps that couldn't be sold in the markets. They were boiled twice (in Shanghai dialect this is called *chuanliang-*

chuan).* The vegetable skins were trucked over to the prison from the markets. Left unpeeled, they were merely boiled in water, after which a pinch of salt was added. There wasn't so much as a drop of oil in them. This completed the "Sichuan dish," infinitely simpler than heating up hog feed.

I didn't feel hungry my first two days there, even though I was unable to stomach the rice and the "Sichuan dish." But by the third day I had to eat. I discovered that the rice was a trifle better than it had been that time at Caohejing Prison; at least it didn't taste of kerosene. Unfortunately, though, after only a few mouthfuls you hit bottom. There wasn't much food in the iron containers. All sixteen people in the room agreed, "You can never eat your fill here."

"As the saying goes," said one young prisoner, "there are capital offenses, but there are no crimes for which punishment is starvation. Starvation is harder to bear than death!"

The food was brought in a little after four o'clock, and by seven in the evening your stomach would begin beating the gong. When I was so hungry that my vision blurred, I would habitually look for edible insects on the floor, even if all I found was a green beanbug. But there weren't any reeds† here; I couldn't find anything. However, I did find bedbugs in the cracks in the floor. At times like these I thought with sweet recollection of the chewing gum and coffee Wang Lei had given us, and I remembered with relish eating grasshoppers and green larvae. I even cherished the memory of over forty years before in Number Two Model Prison when I was so hungry I stuck my hand into the small cloth bag for peanuts.

The prisoners began to look like skin and bones. The light in their eyes was also strange, a kind of slow, gray look that exhibited total greed.

Chuan is how the Shanghainese pronounce the Mandarin word *gun*, meaning "to boil," and *liang* means "twice" here.

†Literally, *xingtiaolin*, a kind of hemp used to weave baskets, referring here to a plant found in the area in which the author was lost in Shandong in part 2.

One method the inmates thought up for curing hunger was "spiritual dining." Each prisoner would describe how to make a famous dish or snack. All the great foods of Yangzhou, Sichuan, Guangdong, and Shanghai were divided by type and described carefully in great detail. During the explanation, even the sound of the oil popping in the wok and the color, smell, and taste of the food after it was cooked were vividly evoked. The speaker brought the listeners to such a state that we all salivated.

When we were through talking about famous dishes we devised a new way to "spiritually dine." We recalled how many food stalls there were in the City God Temple area of Shanghai. Old Shanghainese could tick them off in order starting from the temple gate entrance without missing a one—like counting the family's jewels. Then another Shanghai hand would add the price of each kind of food. Thus we whiled away the long days but, more importantly, appeased our hunger nerves. Once another Shanghainese said he could name all the restaurants and snack shops on Nanjing Road between the Bund and Jing'an Temple. My hunger finally became unbearable. "Come on, don't talk about it!" I said. "The more you talk about it the more we want it, and the more we want it, the hungrier we get, and the hungrier we get, the more we want our freedom. Just forget it!" This outburst of mine signaled an end to our "spiritual dining."

This third bout of starvation differed from both the time in Number Two Model Prison and the time in the brush at Lijinwa. Here, our bellies weren't completely empty. Instead, we were kept half alive. They gave us enough to titillate and tease our appetite, but never enough to eat our fill, only one-third of the amount needed to satisfy our appetite. Hunger like this was particularly insufferable: your mouth gave off not a bitter taste, but a sour one; your belly was always growling and your nerves were on edge. Gradually your hands and feet grew numb and listless, and the pink on your nails faded little by little until all the blood coloration disappeared. Even your hair turned to sparse, withered grass from the length of time in prison.

The "wisdom" of Old Zhang, the "nutrition specialist" locked up with me in the old days, turned out to be very useful now. He once said that in circumstances where nutrition is inadequate it is best to "increase income and reduce expenditure." "Increasing income" meant devising a way to get hold of something more to eat. "Reducing expenditures" meant doing your best to conserve energy. He said that every extra sentence spoken consumed calories. Locked up in this "dead end" there just wasn't any "income" to increase. All I could do was "reduce expenditures" by not moving around much or speaking, much like a sitting Buddha. Based on this principle, I advised the young people newly arrived not to do push-ups or early morning exercises along with the radio.

Another method was to lead the brain's thoughts away from one's stomach to forget the brutal reality of hunger. This was just the opposite of "spiritual dining." One time we made a resolution that during the next twenty-four hours no one would talk about anything related to food, and that anyone who violated this rule would be penalized by getting one less spoonful to eat at mealtime. As you can imagine, a punishment like this was more severe than a twenty-stroke beating. The goal of this "legislation" was to make everyone forget his hunger, but in fact, everybody became even more caught up in it, and the resulting torment was even greater. Why? The problem lay in the threat of the loss of the spoonful of food.

Playing chess and making up riddles can also distract you from hunger, but you can only come up with so many riddles in a day, and we were not allowed to play chess.

Of course, reading—beneficial in itself— is the best method for curing hunger. It was our extreme misfortune that the people then in power, Wang Weiguo and his ilk, were savages using "ignorance" to rule the nation. They were hostile to all human culture, viewing it as "feudal," "capitalistic," or "revisionist," and they forbade us to read anything but *Mao's Selected Works* and the Little Red Book. We had read this book I don't know how many times and had it down pat, so it no longer aroused our interest. This reminds me of how I'd obtained my education. I was an elementary school graduate and attended half a year of middle school before going to work in a factory. Ironically, it was in the Guomindang jail that I had had the opportunity to read many books (I read several hundred of the "Universal Library Series" published by Commercial Press) and to study Japanese with Comrade Xu Yushu. It would not be inaccurate to say that prison had been my "university." And yet now, under the name of "military rule," public security jails only permitted prisoners to take one course—a course in "hunger."

III

Detention quarters were used as temporary "storehouses" for handling criminals of all kinds. One group would be arrested and locked up for a time, then another would be sentenced to the Tilanqiao Prison or a labor reform camp. Those known as "idle goods" were detained here for a long time, some for as long as ten or twenty years. Without being sentenced or released, they remained "prisoners awaiting trial." If you asked what law they had broken, they uttered nothing. During the Cultural Revolution everything was abnormal. The offenders in this temporary storehouse were already packed as densely as sardines in a can. Even though people were moved in and out of the cells, those coming in always outnumbered those taken out. As a result, when we lay huddled together on the floor at night, if someone had to get up to relieve himself he would wake up the whole chain of people around him. What's worse, the light in the cell was on all night, and your empty stomach didn't let you sleep, either. Though I had been through two other bouts with "near starvation" and my body was somewhat used to this, it revealed its decay and uselessness during this third encounter. The worst problem was that I couldn't sleep, and the more I was unable to sleep, the more I felt the intolerable hunger. In my anger all I could do was pull the quilt up over my head to block out the bleak green light that glowed through the night. But the quilt made me break out in a cold sweat from head to toe. Then "richly endowed" bedbugs coming out from the cracks in the floor would suck blood from every part of me. All my wrath was channeled into the battle to kill them. I would pick up my pillow (in reality it was my rubber shoes) and press ruthlessly with the soles, then continue to rub the floor several times. I thus wiped out hordes of bedbugs, but this victory produced a nauseating odor.

Staring at the ceiling at night when I couldn't sleep, I would see bedbugs dropping down from the cracks. They were truly devilish; they would take aim and always fall on the uncovered part of the person sleeping below. There was nothing I could do about the ones on the ceiling.

No matter how much I tried "decreasing expenditures," my body was still clearly deteriorating, and I knew that the roots of my weakness were the loss of sleep, hunger, and masses of blood-sucking bedbugs. We heard that the district epidemic prevention station had at one time shown concern for our health and issued some powder to exterminate the bugs. But the powder had never made it here because it was poisonous and could provide a convenient opportunity for us to commit suicide. Thus, we revised Wang Weiguo's slogan to say: "Mercy toward bedbugs is cruelty toward political prisoners!"

As I stared at the dismal light in the room, waiting for the first rays of morning sun gradually showing beyond the window, I realized that I was striding rapidly toward death and bemoaned the fact that I was not born at the right time. Why did so much appalling suffering befall my generation?

Motherland, plagued by heavy disasters, seventeen years after revolutionary victory, how could you have the heart to put your loyal sons and daughters through a blood bath of untold danger once again?

I had already been through two devastating bouts with hunger. How could it be that this great land, for which I struggled with sweat and blood, could so savagely torture its beloved son? Is this regime worthy of being called a dictatorship of the proletariat? Is this kind of Communist Party worthy of being called an organization of the proletarian vanguard?

Today another new prisoner was brought in, 1288. His number indicated there were already more than 1,200 people in this concentration camp. The new criminal was about fifty years old. His face and manner revealed a cultured, high-level intellectual. The only thing that displeased us about him was his obesity—we were already packed tight enough together on the floor at night. A colossus like him, who occupied the space of two people, was definitely not welcome.

No. 1288 was like a man without a soul; his dull eyes were full of despair. He was expressionless and showed absolutely no interest in his surroundings. It was as if he had not yet recovered from a dreadful shock. He wore leather shoes. To keep the room clean, one had to remove one's shoes upon entering. He complied, and sat down on the floor.

"What is this place?" he finally asked after the longest time.

"Jail."

He looked surprised. "Oh! Are there prisons as nice as this?" Everybody thought he was joking. "What do you find nice about this place?" they asked.

"There's a glass window and a floor, and the floor is so clean!" he replied, pointing to the glass window at the back.

"How many times have you been in prison before?" asked the inmates, trying to draw him out.

"Twice."

I thought to myself that this guy wasn't so simple after all.

No. 1207 derided him. "You must be an old counterrevolutionary, huh!"

"This is the first time I've been indicted by the Communist Party," said 1288, defending himself.

"What about the other time, then?"

"I went to America when I was young. Because my papers weren't complete, actually because they looked down on the yellow race, they put me in a dark immigration prison. I was locked up a full eleven days. That prison was much worse than this—the floor was concrete, and it didn't have any windows. If I have to be in prison, I'd rather come back and be in one here.'' He spoke earnestly, with no sarcasm.

"Well, do inmates in America eat their fill?'' somebody asked.

"They eat bread there, not rice. You can always get filled up on bread.''

"Okay, in a few days you'll be able to make an accurate comparison.''

I was especially happy to have an English teacher delivered to my doorstep like this. I asked him to teach me and the others English. He, too, was most enthusiastic. He wrote down new vocabulary on our teaching material—toilet paper—but after only two classes, Old Cai (1207) criticized us.

"This is no the place to study English. If somebody reports you and says you're propagating Western culture, wouldn't that just add to your crimes?''

Old Cai meant well by his suggestion. It was best to stop the English lessons.

From then on Old Cai was nicknamed "Emergency Brake.'' He was a cellist from the conservatory, and we didn't know what he had been brought in for. I figured he'd probably once belonged to a rebel group because of his familiarity with the rebel groups' methods of interpreting everything one did as a political statement. Since we weren't familiar with the rules and taboos of the new people in power, people like "Emergency Brake'' were still needed, so everyone respected him.

When somebody asked 1288 to talk about what things were like in America, he responded, "I can talk even less about *that*. Whether I say it was good or bad, either way I'd be propagating capitalism and making the number one enemy look good. Right? The rebels have already labeled me an American spy.''

From this I realized that the main reason he was in prison this time was that he had studied in the United States. At the time, studying abroad was a crime.

On 1288's second day, someone realized he was a famous surgeon. Fellow inmate He Longjiang's father had once contracted tuberculosis and had two ribs removed in an operation at the Chest Hospital. The doctor who did the operation was none other than 1288—Gu Guanshi. He Longjiang had seen Dr. Gu on the day of his father's operation. When Dr. Gu was identified there was great excitement, since he was praised all over the city as the "Number Two Knife in Shanghai," meaning that his surgical skills were the second best in the city. Never in a million years would I have thought that such a famous surgeon would be locked up here.

Once He Longjiang revealed his identity, Dr. Gu grew ashamed and uneasy.

The regulations in this place made us use a number for identification; no one was allowed to use his real name. For those with some degree of reputation and who were concerned about their self-respect, it was a handy means of covering up their real identity, enabling them to maintain a measure of intellectual dignity even in prison. Now that He Longjiang had ripped away this protective covering, the public knew that Dr. Gu was a counter-revolutionary, and this brought the doctor great misery.

Once the curtain masking Dr. Gu had been pulled open, other secrets gradually came to light. The real crime that got him "promoted" to prison was a great medical breakthrough he had made. He was the first surgeon to experiment with Chinese acupuncture as an anesthetic during surgery. In April that year an old schoolmate had returned from abroad to visit him. Dr. Gu told him about his medical achievement but shouldn't have, because the man went back and told people about the great discovery in Chinese medicine. How was he to know that his praise of New China would land his friend Dr. Gu in prison?

China's system of maintaining secrets is unique. Everything must be kept secret, yet nobody knows just what constitutes a "state secret." Thus it is very easy to violate the law by divulging state secrets. During those terrifying years, besides the widespread unjust charges of being a traitor or spy, and of attacking the red sun [Chairman Mao], the accusations "divulger of state secrets" and "maintainer of illicit relations with foreign countries" flew thick and fast. Dr. Gu's crime was divulging state secrets.

Three days later, Dr. Gu, too, began to feel hungry. "I still have a rich accumulation of fatty tissue under my skin," he said. "My brain will redistribute all the essential nutritive elements in my body." After two weeks, however, he too had clearly grown thinner. The pants he wore when he came in were now one or two inches too big. Two months later he was nearly as thin as I was, his face showing many wrinkles, the kind you get from losing a lot of weight fast. This benefited the group, since it meant less crowding at night.

One day he picked up a metal lunch container and discovered a small bit of toilet paper in the "Sichuan dish." How cruel a punishment for a doctor who was meticulous about hygiene! In agony, he firmly pushed his lunch container away and used hot water to wash his spoon over and over, lest it be infected with germs. Yang the Sixth was sitting at his side. "Why aren't you eating?" he asked 1288.

"How could I eat something like *this*?"

"If you don't eat the vegetables, at least eat the rice."

"Germs can spread."

"Didn't you say that boiling kills the germs?"

"Theoretically, yes. But there's no way I can eat that."

Consequently, Yang the Sixth, as if finding treasure, transferred Dr. Gu's food into his own bowl. He was a little bit sheepish about it. Perhaps feeling selfish, he divided out a portion and gave it to me. "I don't mind that it might be unsanitary, but I don't want it." I said. "Give it to the young people." He took the rest and gave it to the two prisoners next to him. Consoling himself as he ate, Yang said, "What the eyes can't see is clean! The fact is, they've never picked out the bad stuff from the food for our cell. The whole pot could be infected with this type of thing. Who cares? Survival is the important thing!"

One of the others who had received a portion of the food

rejoiced, "Even if it's full of dirt, still my stomach it can't hurt!" The others who hadn't received any looked with jealousy and envy at Yang and the other two.

An idea suddenly flashed through my mind. Could I make use of my resistance experience in the Guomindang jail to organize these prisoners to launch a hunger strike? If so, we could propose four conditions to the prison authorities: (1) prisoners' grain rations should be increased; (2) meals should be improved, oil should be added to the food, and sanitary food should be guaranteed; (3) prisoners should not be beaten and cursed; and (4) relatives must be allowed to bring in food. But this notion dissipated as quickly as it had formed because I realized that no matter how deplorable the management of this prison, in the final analysis it still belonged to the "dictatorship of the proletariat," and if we really went on a hunger strike, wouldn't we be resisting our own class dictatorship? And wouldn't this add yet another "counter-revolutionary" charge to my indictment? Besides, these prisoners didn't compare with the others back then—all genuine, authentic CCP members. The people locked up here included some who'd been involved with the rebels, some old cadres who had been framed, and some good, honest, but timid ordinary members of the community. Everyone came with a different point of view, so ideological unity would be impossible. If by chance there emerged one or two people who tried to inform on us to gain leniency for themselves, I would really be drawing fire on myself.

Another idea worked more powerfully against my first "impulse." The warden in the Guomindang prison had been afraid that prisoners dying from a hunger strike would adversely affect his official position. But these counterfeit Communist security people had no qualms about doing exactly as they pleased. Their prisoners were no more than ants to them. If you fasted, that just saved on food. If a few prisoners died, those "revolutionaries" wouldn't even raise an eyebrow!

It was on this evening that a young man in our cell, 1296, went to the back corner to relieve himself and violently struck his head against the cement corner of the "squathole." The knee-high cement "squathole" was built over the hole dug in the corner for going to the bathroom. This young guy was suddenly banging his head against the cement to end his short life! The noise immediately woke everybody. Old Cai went swiftly to the doorway to report it to the guard. I quickly picked up the youth, who by now had a face full of blood. 1288, the brilliant surgeon who just happened to have been put in our cell, immediately sprang up, tore off a strip of material from his pants, and bound the head wound. But the youth pushed 1288 away, saying weakly, "Don't bother. Death is the best way out. I can't face Teacher Xie. . . . " What did he mean? Nobody knew, but as long as we could hear him talk clearly we knew he was still alive and were relieved.

Half an hour went by before the guard finally opened the door. When he saw that 1296's head had been well wrapped, he pulled him out of the room, screaming viciously, "Is *this* suicide? If you were looking to die, why didn't you? You're just using death to resist the dictatorship of the proletariat! Yeah, we've seen a lot of this. Every day more than a few die—but don't think it's possible to shake our proletarian power!"

No one slept the rest of the night. All sorts of thoughts stirred in our minds. It wasn't easy to reveal one's anger to any of the others. Dr. Gu was the only one to talk. "I've contemplated death before, too. For a doctor, there are many ways available. But I have a wife at home, and if she knew I'd died in here without knowing why, she'd have an even harder time of it. So I don't do it!"

"Did your wife return with you from America?" I asked.

This question opened him up. His eyes filling with tears, he replied softly, "Yes. She was my girlfriend. I met her at school in the United States. We've been married nineteen years. Abroad, we were discriminated against everywhere. During the McCarthy era in America, all the Chinese there became targets of the FBI and suffered all kinds of hardships and bullying. When we heard that the motherland had become strong and had even fought American troops in Korea, each and every one of us overseas felt proud and elated. We were already married by then, and I was chief surgeon of a large private hospital. We had a cozy little home and a car, but we preferred to give it all up. We sold all of our property in the United States and rushed back to China in 1954. At that time the CCP still thought highly of people like us. I was appointed director of the Chest Hospital, and my wife became vice-director of the Pharmaceutical Research Institute. But good times don't last long. When the party leadership was replaced by the rebels, they turned against us and not only searched my home, but also confiscated my books and reference materials, as well as our savings. The strangest thing is that my crime this time arose from my medical achievement. If I'd been unambitious and just earned a living, maybe I wouldn't be here. You can't talk reason with these people."

"It looks like you committed the capital crime of disclosing state secrets," I said.

Quite astonished, he replied, "Countries have never kept new medical breakthroughs a secret from one another. This practice is only humanitarian. I don't understand why my talking to a friend back for a visit was a crime."

"Look how naive you are. They could care less about humanitarianism and law! Nowadays, cruelty and barbarism are revolutionary, while it's reactionary to talk about humanitarianism."

Quite hurt, he cried out indignantly, "Is it possible that the motherland my wife and I sought is this savage and lawless nation? . . . Ah, I was blind. I threw myself at the light like a moth attracted to a lamp, only to destroy my life!"

As dawn was breaking, the iron door opened and the guard pushed in the young man who had tried to commit suicide. Unfortunately, they'd handcuffed his hands behind his back as punishment for "using suicide to threaten the dictatorship of the proletariat," and to prevent a second attempt. Though his head was wrapped in new white gauze, his remorseful and timid eyes showed through.

The cellmates were full of sympathy for the youth but spoke to him reproachfully: "Why think of killing yourself? Now they've handcuffed you. You really did it to yourself this time! You're so young, and have so many years ahead of you. . . . ''

With tears, 1296 cried, ''I'm not human—I no longer have a conscience. Teacher Xie loved me so and cared about me . . . I couldn't live with being labeled a 5.16 counterrevolutionary. I incriminated her, I hurt her!''*

His tears rolled down from under the layer of white gauze but his hands were restrained behind his back so he was unable to wipe them away. It came to light that he was an elementary school teacher. Teacher Xie was his wife, or perhaps they hadn't married yet. Under torture he had babbled that she, too, was a 5.16 element. But when he returned to the cell he regretted it, and his conscience led him to suicide.

''As long as you're alive there will always be a day when you can clear this thing up.'' I said. ''If you die, your Teacher Xie will be a 'counterrevolutionary' forever. Wouldn't that hurt her all her life? You see how foolish your behavior is?''

He was silent for a while and then said, ''I really want to die. Death is the best way to end all my problems.''

''Don't think such things. You should have faith in our New China.'' The fact was, though, that I felt as insecure as he did.

''If you'd left me alone just now, it would have been all right!'' he responded.

This really got to Dr. Gu. ''Nowadays everything is upside down,'' he laughed bitterly. ''People complain if you save their lives, they want to die when they have someone who loves them, and it's a crime to have made a contribution to society. Good people turn bad, and I—the fat man—turn into a stick!''

Having your hands cuffed behind your back is a very cruel

---

*Author's note: ''5.16'' refers to the ''May 16 Directive'' drafted by Mao Zedong, called ''5.16'' for short. Later the ''Gang of Four'' fabricated a story that there was a counterrevolutionary group called ''5.16'' and the whole country launched a movement to nab ''5.16 elements,'' using forced letters of confession and torture to implicate hundreds of thousands of people. At the time the crime of being a ''5.16 element'' was equivalent to being a counter-revolutionary opposing Chairman Mao.

punishment. You can't pull down your pants to relieve yourself, you have to gnaw at your food like a dog or a pig, and you have to sleep with your back to the ceiling. . . . This bunch had lost their humanity; here was someone who had just tried to kill himself, and they were using methods even more brutal because of it. What kind of devil's brew could produce such barbarous, inhumane "revolutionaries"?

That same evening, after everyone had fallen asleep, I was suddenly awoken by a pitiful cry coming from next to me. I sat up quickly and saw the elementary school teacher, hands locked behind his back, bent over the squathole. I realized immediately that this was his second suicide attempt. With his hands fastened behind him, he stood on top of the hole, leapt full-body into the air, and rammed his head onto the cement below, using the weight of his body to smash against the concrete. Everyone was startled awake. Dr. Gu went over to lift him up and found blood still flowing from his nose and mouth. On his forehead was an inch-long gash. His pained, blurred eyes were still open, still shining in a face covered with blood. His bloody head rested on Dr. Gu's arm and his weak voice was barely audible. "Don't bother, let me die." When he finished speaking, more blood came from his mouth. My first thought was that my advice to go on living had been futile. Heartless rulers had driven him to death. His last ounce of hope was gone. . . .

Dr. Gu's rescue was wasted; the pitiful youth had reached his objective. His beautiful sparkling eyes (I discovered that a dying person's eyes are especially beautiful) closed—very, very slowly.

As before, it was Old Cai who went to the doorway and screamed, "Guard! There's been an accident!" The guard walked over with sleepy eyes. Hearing that a prisoner had committed suicide, he looked at the door for a while and then, without the least bit of concern, said, "We'll talk about it at five A.M. Carry the body over here by the door."

"The dead man still has handcuffs on," said Old Cai, standing at the door. "Can't you take them off first?"

With the same indifferent expression, the guard swore, "You

son of a bitch! My orders are that the cell door doesn't open before five A.M. You got that?''

We dragged the corpse to the side of the prison door. His hands were still slightly warm, the glittering KLM electroplated handcuffs cutting into them. He carried with him humiliation, unfulfilled love, the scars of forced confession, and the censure of his own weakness. He buried himself in resistance against the tyranny of the Middle Ages that prevailed here. Perhaps Old Cai was a Christian. He begged the guard to take off the handcuffs, maybe to let the dead man's soul fly up to heaven that much sooner. This unclarified wish was never realized. As far as I'm concerned, once someone is dead, handcuffs won't add to his suffering; his hands may be tightly bound but his soul will not be fettered. The living inhabitants of the cell gathered around the frightening corpse and, sunk in self-pity at our common lot, silently waited for five o'clock.

The waiting seemed endless. Yet I wasn't at all afraid of looking at the dead man because I had seen him alive and had watched how he died. Though there was a lot to say, not a word was uttered. I imagine everybody wanted to say the same thing but was afraid lest they disturb the hapless youth. So we remained silent. At the time, a million thoughts welled up inside me. I wondered what had become of his love, Teacher Xie. Since he had incriminated her as a 5.16, she too must be locked up in prison. Could this young man's suicide rescue his lover? If he hadn't died, would Teacher Xie have gone on loving him? What force was it, what sort of "dictatorship" could destroy the union of young lovers and bring a pure and upright young man to his death?

I greatly regretted that I had not striven to understand him better in the last few days and help straighten him out. I didn't even know his wife's name. If I knew her name and the location of her school, as soon as I was free I could look her up and tell her what I knew. But later it occurred to me that since he was already dead, what purpose would talking to her serve, other than adding to her distress and sorrow? My pitiful young man, you really did free yourself of everything. But why didn't you think of your wife?

I noticed that even in death the young man's body was twisted, denied even the freedom of comfort. The shining handcuffs still bound his hands.

Five o'clock came; the sky was still gray. The guard opened the door, and two convict workers came in to haul away the dead man. They dragged him by the feet like a dead dog, his face turned skyward. The iron door shut, and all we heard was the metallic sound of the dead man's handcuffs scraping along the ground. It was a terrible sound, like an iron tool scratching at the pit of my stomach, growing fainter and fainter until it vanished. Only then did I become aware of my silent tears.

After this, talk in the cell naturally centered on whether or not one should commit suicide, and an animated discussion ensued.

The result was that everyone agreed that suicide was an expression of helplessness, and that we should have the will to live on to see the demise of this tragic state, to live on until the day the real world returned to us.

After our talk we cherished our lives even more, and took even better care of ourselves. Everyone agreed to think of ways to get food. This was a struggle to save our lives, and there was no use getting embarrassed about it.

Three days later a doctor came in to see the prisoners, as stipulated in the regulations. Dr. Gu was the first to sign up. Shortly after, a prison doctor in white stood outside the door.

The doctor looked hard at Dr. Gu. "Are you Dr. Gu . . . ?"

Ashamed, Dr. Gu was unwilling to acknowledge who he was. The reversal of roles between teacher and student was awkward for him. But then he realized that admitting who he was might facilitate his getting medicine, so with a bitter smile and no alternative, he nodded.

"You've lost so much weight I hardly recognized you. What's wrong with you? . . . I'll come and look at you this afternoon."

"Thank you. My illness comes from lack of nourishment."

"You've gotten thin, too thin," he said, with sympathy and concern. The young doctor seemed to be the only light in that dark prison.

"It's probably hunger," said Dr. Gu.

That afternoon, the doctor saw 1288 at the door of the cell and gave him a prescription that read, "Allow family members to supply glucose." Beneath this was the clinic stamp. The prison doctor told 1288 at the door, "Give this slip to the person in charge here and write your family's address; have them bring some glucose on their next visit. With this note from the clinic, they'll allow it in." It turned out that Dr. Gu had also taught at Shanghai First Medical College, and his students were all over the country. He couldn't remember this one's name, but on the prescription—worth more than all the gold in the world—was the signature—Wen Dakai.

With the doctor's approval, family members could send in glucose. If this method were equally effective for all the inmates, this could open up a new road out for everyone in the cell. The words "Wen Dakai" appeared like a greatly magnified neon light flashing before our eyes!

IV

Every Thursday a piece of braised pork the size of an ear was added to each prisoner's "Sichuan dish." This jogged my memory. Was this piece of meat the sole reward of our five-day hunger strike forty years ago?

It must have been September 1970; we'd just made it through Wednesday. Everyone was eagerly looking forward to Thursday's piece of meat, each person praying to himself, hoping that his piece of meat would be a little bigger, a little fattier. . . .

Suddenly it was announced that this Thursday no meat would be issued; instead, we would be given one preserved egg apiece. Thus the question of which was better, pork or a preserved egg, became the topic of heated debate. There was unanimous agreement that it would be nice to have a change, but from a nutritional point of view, a preserved egg couldn't beat a piece of meat.

Thursday finally came and we sat in order, one next to the

other. One by one we went up to the door to receive our preserved egg.

Old Cai went to the door to get his, only to discover a smelly
black liquid inside. Straight away the elderly musician looked
despondent. He held the stinking black liquid in his hand, not
knowing what to do. He looked as if he were about to cry.

Quickly, I broke open my egg to try my luck. God! Mine was
still edible. I became a proud prince, at least luckier than
1207. Just then Yang the Sixth, sitting across from me, also
discovered his egg was nothing but a bubble of foul liquid.

I offered a suggestion. "It's not easy to get a piece of meat
once a week, and if you get a spoiled egg like this, which you
can't possibly eat, you can request that the kitchen replace it. It's
a reasonable demand!"

With that encouragement, Old Cai went to the door with his
egg in hand and reported to the guard. When the guard came, the
cellist explained why he wanted to exchange his egg, showing it
to him. The guard sniffed it and left. Soon the head of another
guard appeared outside the door. This was a guy over forty with a
wart under one ear and a Yangzhou accent. "Who was it that just
asked for a new egg?" he yelled from outside the door.

Old Cai instantly went to stand at the doorway, with Yang the
Sixth following behind.

"These are old goods bought cheap," the guard said through
the hole in the door. "We're already giving you special treatment
by feeding you preserved eggs. If *you* don't eat them, who will?
If you want to eat good eggs, just what do you think you're doing
being bad eggs, huh?"

Hearing the guard's tone of voice, Yang the Sixth hurried back
to his place. But the cellist didn't quit. "Everybody's in here for
the same reason. Why should I be the one to get this?"

"Okay, give me your egg," said the guard, unlocking the
door.

When the door opened, the guard pulled him out and smashed
the egg over his head, swearing furiously, "You counterrevolutionary! Rotten egg! You're just the kind of bastard who should

be eating rotten eggs. If you want to eat well, why the hell don't you eat at home? Why come here to be so picky? How can you reform your ideology like this?'' He then cuffed Old Cai across the ears.

When the beating was over, 1207 was shoved through the door covered with black, stinking liquid from his hair to his earlobes, looking like a Peking Opera mask. The putrid smell permeated the room. You could see from his red eyes that he was about to explode, but he didn't say a word.

I was partly to blame for his beating because it was I who suggested that he request a new egg. It was almost as if my face, too, had been hit. Unfortunately, I had already swallowed my egg, or I would have been willing to give it to him as an expression of sympathy. I stood up to wash off his head. It wasn't easy to do because everyone had a limited water ration. For example, if you had two large teacups, you only got four cups of water a day (water was distributed twice daily), and these four cups had to take care of drinking, washing your face, brushing your teeth, cleaning your bowl and spoon, and washing your clothes. A cooperative method was adopted for bathing, water for which was also included in the ration. Several people would gather together to take turns wiping themselves. Thus, each person guarded the water in his own enamel cup like a precious bit of wealth. As I poured out all of my own water to give 1207 to wash off, my cellmates supported me by contributing part of their own savings. This sight moved me as well as the cellist. He hadn't cried during his beating, when his head was made to look like the devil, but now, as everyone in the cell so warmly offered him their water, he wept.

''They can dig out my heart but I won't take part in their damn rebellion!'' he shouted, washing himself off.

Having nothing else to do, we made up a poem about what had happened:

> *Daily we hope for a piece of meat,*
> *Today we got preserved eggs.*

Just a bubble of water inside,
Too stinky to swallow.
Asking for a new egg,
He gave you a cuffing,
"If you want to eat a good egg,
What are you doing in prison?
Since you're a rotten egg,
You should eat rotten eggs!"
A criminal is not human.
The sound of tears is like a flowing spring.

About every two weeks they would drag us downstairs to "air us out" in the small courtyard. The place had four high walls and not a single tree. I noticed scraps of coal piled up at the base of the wall. We haltingly walked around in a hopeless, endless gray circle. Perhaps I was driven by hunger or provoked by my unforgettable experience in the brush, for I began to look inside this small world for insects or other animals. After I had walked four or five times around, I saw a small animal sticking its head out of the coal pile in the corner. I broke rank and sprang at it. It was a toad. My first thought was, is it edible? Time permitted no hesitation; I promptly captured the dull-witted thing gently between my hands. It struggled and sprayed out what I've heard is a poisonous liquid, but I paid no attention to this and hurriedly stuck my hands into my pocket, tightly holding the toad. "What did you catch?" a cellmate asked softly.

"A first-rate meat dish," I answered.

The addition of this one small animal greatly enlivened the dreary, forlorn cell. We got busy. Several people suggested how to deal with the unfortunate amphibian. There was no knife in the cell, but the prisoners kept a needle hidden, which I used as a weapon to slit the toad's skin, easily peeling it off from head to toe.

How could we make the toad more delectable? There were some exceptionally talented and brilliant people in our midst. The idea that someone came up with was to use the flavor from the "Sichuan dish" to salt the toad meat. According to this expert, it would taste even better if you soaked the toad in the salty flavor for two days. But another expert was of the opinion that if there wasn't enough of the marinate, it would go bad the longer it soaked. I ended up listening to the latter and gulped down the toad that very evening. To tell the truth, I really couldn't have waited. It tasted just as good uncooked as cooked.

After this, being "aired out" took on as much significance as the piece of meat we got every Thursday. Everyone combed the courtyard for small animals. But we couldn't expect a toad to show up every time we exercised. One time I saw one, but when I bent down to catch it I discovered it was a cinderball. Many of my companions, too, were tricked into bending over for lumps of coal. We always went out in high spirits and returned disappointed.

In our efforts to overcome our hunger, another "inventor" stepped forward. He was He Longjiang, a student of German at the Foreign Languages Institute. His father, who had been operated on by Dr. Gu, was a veteran cadre who had been district party secretary. They say he was arrested for offending the old man [Mao] by using thumbtacks to hang up his sacred portrait. Like the evil intentions of Auntie Zhao when she pricked the paper figures of Jia Baoyu and Wang Xifeng in *Dream of the Red Chamber*, this was a very serious offense. He Longjiang was young, and his grain ration outside prison had been large. Here it was the young ones who most felt the threat of starvation. In a moment of desperation he thought up the idea of squeezing toothpaste into his food tin. After mixing, it really did somewhat resemble creamed rice. In color, smell, and taste it wasn't bad. I've eaten rice mixed with toothpaste myself. It has a unique flavor.

Family members were permitted to provide us with toothpaste, soap, toilet paper, and towels every month, so a source of toothpaste was guaranteed. Thereafter, the idea of "creamed rice" spread rapidly, and lots of us squeezed toothpaste into our rice.

Dr. Gu did not think highly of this discovery. According to

him, toothpaste contained talcum powder and a chemical preparation of soap suds, neither of which was good for digestion. He said it actually reduced the amount of time the food stayed in your stomach, making it even easier to feel hungry. Thus opened an academic debate over the eating of toothpaste.

He Longjiang gave rein to his thesis. If we eat toothpaste it should be high quality because high-quality toothpaste has glycerine, a valuable nutrient. Then when we eat "creamed rice" our stomachs will absorb the glycerine and reject the chemical soap preparation and talcum powder. We'd reach a balance, with body "income" offsetting "expenditures." As to how much more we'd gain, there was no way to calculate that at the moment, but in this deadly place, getting even a little more than the allotted nutrients was beneficial.

He Longjiang's scientific exposition and his ability to bring together the practical features of the discussion left Dr. Gu speechless. In the end it fell on me to effect a compromise.

"Dr. Gu's reasoning is correct," I said. "It's harmful to eat regular toothpaste. High-quality toothpaste is for prisoners. We all know that astronauts in satellites eat 'toothpaste' too!* This is like a satellite here—a tiny place completely isolated from the rest of the world. We can't see our families or write them. And if one of our spare parts breaks down, we'll plunge to our deaths in space, and people on earth will hold a grand burial ceremony for our ashes."

V

There was another high-ranking person in our cell, 1236. At the beginning no one knew what he did on the outside, or what his name was. Where we were, the higher someone's position, the less willing he was to divulge his status. Dr. Gu had been like that.

---

*Author's note: Astronauts use as food a liquid with extremely high nutritive value that is put into toothpaste tubes, thus the analogy.

Though 1236 had landed in prison just like us, he had some habits that were out of the ordinary. Before going to sleep he always folded his clothes and socks very neatly, especially his pair of woolen pants, always managing to press the seams. Every morning he washed out his handkerchief, and the white-collared shirt he wore was somehow always washed clean and worn neatly, despite the scarcity of water here.

His family provided him with as many as five or six tea mugs of various sizes. Among them was a large one that drew the attention of 1274, who was a worker in the Jiangnan Shipyard. He scrutinized the printing on the mug, "Tianzhang Joint State-Private Woolen Mill," and below this, the number "0002."

How familiar the sight of this mug was to 1274! His wife was a veteran worker in that same mill. They had a mug just like this at home, and the cup assigned to his wife was, coincidentally, "0001." No. 1274 remembered that the Tianzhang factory issued these cups in 1956 when all of the private enterprises in Shanghai were converted into "joint state-private enterprises." The mugs were to commemorate the transformation of the entire industry under joint management. That year his wife was serving as head of the labor union. The union's prestige in the private sector was very high, so the first mug was given to the head of the labor union. Mug no. 2 was issued to the boss of Tianzhang Mill. No. 1274 still remembered: the boss's name was Liu Zhihou, and besides running the mill he also operated a foreign trade company. He was a capitalist of no small means and had served as the vice-chairman of the Association of Industry and Commerce. No. 1274 looked at 1236 with probing eyes. "Could he be the capitalist of Tianzhang Mill?"

And so it was that because of a number on a tea mug, 1236's secret was out.

First 1274 asked him whether or not Tianzhang Mill had a labor chief named Xu Cuidi. From there the two of them started to click like a telephone switchboard circuit connected to the right number. Some people had decided not to say much because of the callousness and darkness of life here. But as soon as the smallest spark of emotion burst forth, once we offered a little more sympathy and warmth to one another, the determination not to talk was destroyed. Secrecy and dignity went out the window. Only because of this did I come to know that our cell contained not only a famous surgeon, but also the vice-chairman of the Shanghai Association of Industry and Commerce, a member of the Municipal Political Consultative Conference, and a capitalist.

What crime had Liu Zhihou committed? I can only describe it briefly. There was a female cadre connected to the Shanghai People's Committee who managed the administration of industry and commerce. It was common for her to have frequent dealings with businesspeople along the Bund. In 1953, falsely using the name of the government, she swindled several wealthy capitalists with some story about the government wanting to set up a factory, for which several million yuan were needed. The government hoped the capitalists would jump at the chance to invest, and they would guarantee the investors' profits. The capitalists recognized the woman as a staff member of the Municipal People's Committee and trusted her. As a result, five or six of them fell into her trap and were defrauded of more than 100,000 yuan. When the government asked her to repay what she had swindled, she only came up with 20,000 yuan, leaving 80,000 of it unaccounted for. So she trumped up stories about people, among them the vice-mayor in charge of culture and education and Liu Zhihou, vice-chairman of the Association of Industry and Commerce, as well as the manager of a big hotel. Altogether, she framed six or seven people, accusing them of dividing among themselves the 80,000 yuan she had temporarily lent them. She told the government that if it wanted to get back the full 100,000 yuan, it would have to get it from them. The government then went to these responsible people to check out the facts, but they all asserted that it was "preposterous and absurd." The People's Court then reached a verdict on the cadre's fabricated incriminations: "It is held that this swindler falsely incriminated innocent people and diverted attention from herself in order to avoid having to repay the amount she had taken." The case had been settled long ago and the swindler punished according to law and locked up in Tilanqiao Prison. Who could have imagined that once the "Gang of Four" overthrew the leadership both inside and outside the party, they would turn up this old debt? Using the imprisoned swindler as their trump card, they swayed public opinion into believing that the six prominent figures originally implicated had actually been involved in the fraud, that it was Liu Shaoqi who covered up for them, and so on. The vice-mayor of Shanghai bore the brunt of the attack and was put in prison first, and then Liu Zhihou was imprisoned for no reason. He said he had never laid eyes on the woman, and that even if he were destitute he wouldn't ask her for money. What a perfect example of sitting at home shut off from the world and having disaster fall on you from out of the blue!

He also said that during his interrogation they never asked him anything about whether or not he had gotten money from the woman. The interrogator concentrated instead on getting him to inform against the nationally renowned vice-mayor.

This morning at the break of dawn the iron door opened. An interrogator came to notify 1236 that today he could leave. Liu Zhihou was overjoyed at this unexpected good news and quickly put his things together. Just as he was about to give his "0002" tea mug to 1274 as a parting gift, the interrogator added from the door, "Don't take your belongings, you'll be coming back." This was a staggering blow to Liu. His excitement cooled instantly. He was numbed, unable to grasp what the man meant. Puzzled, he followed the interrogator out.

Sure enough, when it was nearly nighttime, Liu Zhihou returned and recounted his ordeal.

"Today we're letting you leave in the custody of your family," the interrogator had said to him. "You must return by 5:30 this afternoon." He hadn't waited long before spotting his wife standing beyond the second door. He had permission to leave this way, and the interrogator had given him a "release pass" that allowed him past the main gate. "We're giving you a day of freedom to do whatever you like," he was told.

Why did they give him only one day of freedom? There had to be a catch. Face to face with his wife, from whom he had been separated for over a year, he didn't know where to begin. Her eyes brimmed with tears when she saw him. Like her husband, on this day she too had been struck by excessive joy turned to sudden despair. She was so happy to find out she could see him today, until she learned that she had to have him back to the prison by 5:30. Her joy vanished when she saw her husband, so thin he hardly looked human, his hands so pale they were almost translucent in the sunlight. In this tragic year and a half her life had also been hard. She dared not express her own suffering, her own tears. It was so rare to see her beloved that she just wanted to embrace him and weep bitterly. But she restrained herself, letting the tears remain in her eyes. "How about it?" she asked. "Will you come home with me and have a look? Of course, we lost our original place. We've moved to a small garret."

"No, time is limited. Why go back to a home like that? As soon as I saw it I'd be furious!"

The woman turned her head to see if anyone was tailing them. Liu also turned around to look. Then the two of them crossed the street, again glancing to see if anyone was following. "Why don't they release you? Why only give you one day out?"

"Who knows?" said Liu. "Anyway, there's some reason behind it." He asked her how much money she was carrying; she had over ten yuan.

"Let me eat to my heart's content! They're starving me in there!"

Liu Zhihou saw that opposite them was a snack shop selling wonton and noodles. He walked in, too impatient to wait. "What do you plan to eat?" asked his wife.

"Noodles with meat. In prison I made a vow that the day they let me out the first thing I'd do was eat a bowl of noodles with real fatty meat!"

"Silly! Why eat meat noodles? Why not pick something a little better?" said his wife.

"I can't wait! Noodles with meat *are* the best! Screw them!

Only giving me one day out!'' He decided to sit down and let his wife go buy him the bowl of noodles. As soon as he was served he gulped down the braised pork in one mouthful like a hungry ghost. Taking the rest between his chopsticks, he said in a low voice, ''It's so hard . . . we have to wait seven days just for one piece of meat and even then it's not as big as this.'' He continued eating ravenously, wolfing down a three-ounce bowl of noodles.

''Do they beat you?'' his wife asked.

Liu didn't want to tell her what it was really like because it would make her worry, so he responded calmly, ''It's okay. They haven't beaten me. See?'' He extended his pant leg with its carefully folded straight seam to offer her some assurance.

Seeing how ravenous he was, she couldn't control her tears. ''Do you want to see the kids?''

Liu mulled it over for a moment. ''Let's skip it! Their lives are difficult enough as it is, having a father like me. If I went to see them now, wouldn't it just add to their troubles? . . . Oh, the poor kids!''

Next, his wife took him to a place across from the ''Workers Theater'' for spareribs and glutinous rice-flour cakes. He wanted to eat two portions, but his wife cautioned, ''Leave a little room. Have something different to eat.'' Liu licked his lips, walked out of the restaurant, and patted his stomach. ''You just don't know. I'm so hungry my stomach is like a bottomless pit. It'll hold whatever I put into it.''

''I've heard that starving people shouldn't eat too much at once,'' said his wife. ''Be careful not to make yourself sick.''

Liu Zhihou walked along the bustling sidewalk with his wife, eating his way from one restaurant to the next. Beginning to feel replenished, he lifted his head to gaze at the sky illuminated by the bright sun and felt how glorious the world was, and how gentle and considerate his wife was. Though they'd been married for over twenty years, today their love had reached a peak previously unknown. Today, for the first time, he discovered her strong points, points never before revealed. It was today, too, that for the first time he saw her real beauty. ''It is for this that I will never kill myself!'' he said to himself, as he turned his head to look up at the big clock above the racecourse. Already it mercilessly pointed to 11:20. ''Time is running out.''

Seeing his anxious face, she asked solicitously, ''Tell me, how do they treat you in there? This case of yours is obviously unjust. When will they finally clear it up?''

Finding a way to console himself, he replied, ''Being locked up in there has one advantage. There are no classes among the inmates; everybody's the same. Surprisingly, there's no prejudice against me in there for being a capitalist.''

''Then how will your case be settled?''

''It's sad that our nation has no laws. They arrest people as they like and lock up a criminal for seven or eight years. We're just like poultry in a cage; if they want to kill us, keep us cooped up . . . our fates are entirely in their hands. But in the last three years there's been a trend: the greater one's contribution to the country, the greater one's social prestige, or the higher one's position in the party, the more serious the crime. See how many people from the party's Central Committee have been overthrown? Even the mayor and vice-mayor of Shanghai haven't been let off. It's considered unimportant what law they broke. My case can't be too serious because I'm not a leading official within the party, and I rank only fourth in line among the vice-chairmen of the Association of Industry and Commerce. When the interrogator was questioning me, he didn't say a word about what crime I'd committed. He just wanted me to provide information on the vice-mayor. They're probably using me as a weapon with which to attack other people. I'm not a principal player, so you can stop worrying.''

After 12:00 the clock seemed to speed up. It was already 2:30 and they had crossed only a few more streets. How Liu Zhihou wished he could eat a year's supply of food in one day. Again he started going into snack shops, and then went for some Western food. Just after 5:00, even though his ''bottomless pit'' had reached its limit, he went into ''Meixin's'' to have a plate of sauteed shrimp and drink some wine. After he had eaten, he patted his bulging belly. "I'm truly happy to be a cow-devil," he said. "Isn't it the truth?" his wife responded. "Even though you're locked up in the 'cowshed,' I still get to see you."

"I *would* like to be a cow-devil," said Liu Zhihou, smiling. "An animal that chews its cud gets full quickly."

As 5:30 drew closer, Liu's wife grew more and more unsettled. It was as if the Grim Reaper were following her husband, forcing him to the guillotine.

"Only fifteen minutes left!" his wife almost cried out in alarm, after which two streams of hot tears trickled down her face.

This struck Liu like a bolt of lightning. Hiccuping, he said, "Then let me go back. Take care of yourself, my love! Teach the kids to resign themselves to adversity."

"No, I want to accompany you inside and hand you over to them." Then she suggested, "Can we buy a little more to eat? Something you can carry in with you to eat later?"

Suddenly he remembered all his cellmates crying out for food. Since he was able to enjoy a day out, he should think of a way to carry in something good for them. But these feelings for his friends in adversity came to him only five minutes before he had to return. Time didn't allow him to be choosy. He rushed over to a small shop not far from the detention center and bought a dollar's worth of candy. Other kinds of food would bulge in his pockets and wouldn't be easy to slip in. He distributed the candy among his shirt and pants pockets.

Fortunately, no one searched him before he reentered the cell. He carried in just under half a *jin* of assorted candies. He fished it out from his pockets and put it on the floor, and announced that, based on the number of people, each person could have five pieces. Liu Zhihou was like a savior from heaven.

The pitiful prisoners, mouths full of candy, looked upon the profusion of colorful candy wrappers like rare objects of art to be collected, when Old "Emergency Brake" Cai pointed out that we should quickly throw the wrappers down the toilet. It was against the rules to bring in candy, and if the wrappers were found by the guards, it would stir up more trouble. With that, every last wrapper was thrown away.

Everyone in the cell envied Liu Zhihou. Dr. Gu said, "It would make me happy to have just half a day to see if my wife is dead or alive."

Sitting beside me was a man from Shandong who didn't open his mouth much. After he had finished his candy, he, too, spoke. "If only they would give me an hour of freedom and let me go home to see if everything's all right."

"Why do you think the interrogator let you out for a day?" asked some cellmates.

"I'm still not clear," replied Liu Zhihou. "Maybe they want to soften me up. If they want to get me to implicate others in criminal activity, this sort of trick is worse than a forced confession."

"How do you plan to deal with them?" asked He Longjiang.

"I just won't report on anybody. This way I can get them to let me out a couple more times and eat my fill. And I can carry back a little candy for you again."

VI

Sitting next to me was another mystery man, the one from Shandong who had said, "If only they would give me an hour of freedom. . . . " when Liu brought in the candy. He was a big man, 1073. Though we had lived together a long time now, I had not yet probed into the details of his life, as he'd been tight-lipped all along. And it was only because I had spent five or six years in Shandong and could speak a little Shandong dialect that we were on relatively good terms. We would talk about things like the scenery in his native province and the difference between western Shandong and Bohai.

Although regulations didn't permit a prisoner in custody to see his family, family members were allowed to send in daily articles once a month. Besides toothpaste, toothbrushes, toilet paper, changes of clothing, and the like, scraps of material to patch clothes were also permitted. One time 1073 received these daily articles and several odds and ends of material. I noticed among them a worn-out, faded scrap from a military uniform. That particular kind of military material was handwoven by the local women of a wartime revolutionary base. I, too, had worn that uniform during the war. Seeing it now brought back scenes of chaos and destruction during the Anti-Japanese War. From this pile of scraps I deduced that he was a veteran cadre who had participated in the revolution early on. What amazed me was that when he saw these ends of material, this towering, hefty man from Shandong began to cry. Only then did I realize that there was a side to him that could be easily upset. I took advantage of the situation, hoping to get at his personal secrets. I asked softly:

"What's the matter? This brings back memories to me, too!" Only then did he become aware of his tears, and quickly wiped them away, saying nothing. I picked up the scrap of brown military cloth. "This cloth is at least twenty-five years old. It ought to be in a museum. It's had a glorious past, hasn't it?"

"You should be an archaeologist," he said, impressed by my insight. He picked out another remnant from a pair of knitted trousers and threw it in front of me. "Can you figure out where this came from?"

I fingered the piece of cotton trouser material, checking it out closely. They were children's pants, for a child of about five or six, and a name was embroidered on them in colored thread at the waist—"Zhou Xinguo." This was a big find, for I knew from this that the last name of the child's father was Zhou, and that his mother's embroidery was meticulous and that she must be a good mother. I knew, too, why 1073 had been unable to control his tears over this scrap of material.

"These are the cotton pants your son wore when he entered kindergarten, and your wife embroidered his name on them to keep them from getting mixed up with the others'. Right?"

He acknowledged this by smiling slightly and nodding his head. "That son of mine won't do his homework when I'm not home. He's nearly graduated from junior high school by now. I have a daughter, too. She works hard. I don't know how my family's doing.''

''Whom do you miss most, your daughter or her mother?''

''I miss them both. But my wife may be in the same situation as me, locked up some place. Maybe my son sent these things in.''

''What's your wife's problem?''

''Her class background isn't very good. She's a veteran cadre, a capitalist roader . . . ,'' he replied, opening the secrets of his heart a crack.

''Did we struggle all these years for our entire families to be put in prison?'' I responded, furious.

''Don't complain.'' He criticized me angrily. ''This revolution was launched by the old man himself!'' He glanced cautiously around the room, silently signaling to see if anyone had overheard.

Although I had advanced a step in my understanding of him, the door was about to shut tightly. I realized that he was politically more experienced than I. Even though he was a bit younger, he was like an older brother giving me timely, stern, and wellmeaning advice. ''You're really something,'' he said to me quietly. ''Do you know where we are? This is an organ of the dictatorship. Even if you haven't committed a crime they'll dig one up for you. You're awfully loose with words. Are you trying to add more counterrevolutionary crimes to your indictment?''

''What did I say? I don't remember a thing.'' My face reddened.

''That's how careless you are.'' He sighed. ''You blunder over and over again but don't draw any lesson from it! You told 1288 this place was a concentration camp. What effect do you think talk like that has?''

Suddenly I remembered the time when Old Cai was beaten up because of the rotten egg and I had said that in anger. I couldn't help but feel deep respect for this Zhou. I admired his caution. Again he spoke. ''Think about it. You also said something that could be interpreted as a political statement.''

''What else have I said?'' I asked quite timidly, thoroughly ashamed.

"You said, 'Everything is upside down.' If someone were to report you, wouldn't that count as another criminal act?''

I tried to defend myself. "But what I said is a fact, it's the truth! Dr. Gu's said the same thing.''

"You old fool! It's not in vogue now to speak the truth. Don't you know that yet? Dr. Gu isn't a party member, but we are. We should uphold and protect the party's prestige wherever we are!''

"Do you mean to say that we should rely on lies to maintain the party's reputation?'' He said nothing, but blinked painfully.

Having had this confidential talk, our degree of intimacy and mutual trust surpassed that of our cellmates.

The next time relatives were allowed to send in provisions, Dr. Gu got a package of glucose as expected. When he broke open the plastic bag and spooned it out, the eyes of everyone in the room lit up. Dr. Gu became quickly aware of this and politely and generously offered to give each person one tablespoon, following the example of 1236, who had distributed candy to everyone after his day out. But we were embarrassed to accept such a gift. "How could we eat your nutriment?'' I said. "The doctor prescribed it for *you*." But in private I asked him to do me a favor and get in touch with Dr. Wen to see if he could also give me a saving prescription. Dr. Gu promised that when Dr. Wen came in to examine us he would say something to him. At almost the same time, 1073, too, asked Dr. Gu for help. He said he felt a little pain around his liver area and hoped that he could get some glucose or cod liver oil pills. Dr. Gu rubbed the man's right rib area and said with alarm, "You've got a swollen liver. It's five fingers big. See the doctor immediately. Glucose can help what you've got, so you should take more.''

One afternoon two days later, Dr. Wen came to the door, "Anyone have anything wrong?''

I quickly ran up to the door. "I'm sick. I sweat abnormally at night, and my gums bleed all the time. . . .'' According to Dr. Gu's instructions, I listed some other vital symptoms. Then 1073 also came up to the door. Dr. Gu stuck his head out to tell his student, "That prisoner you talked with just now—his nutrition

is seriously inadequate. . . .'' Before he went on, Dr. Wen understood and before long passed a prescription to me. Next, 1073
pressed closer to let Dr. Wen reach out to feel his swollen liver
area, and it wasn't long before 1073 was given the same prescription. Both of us had an inexpressible feeling of gratitude for Dr.
Wen.

When I saw this prescription, which would allow glucose and
cod liver oil to be delivered to us, I was so happy I nearly burst
into tears. I immediately wrote a letter notifying my family that
they were to buy two packages of glucose and two bottles of cod
liver oil pills (these amounts being the maximum regulations
permitted) for their next delivery. I attached the prescription that
had Dr. Wen's signature on it and handed it to the guard.

Of course, 1073 did the same. Without meaning to, I glanced
at the envelope attached to the letter he had written home and
discovered that it said "To Comrade Wang Lei." My heart
skipped a beat! "Is this the Wang Lei I know?" I thought again,
"Could there be another woman with the same name?" When I
remembered the name on his son's kindergarten pants—Zhou
Xinguo—I was certain. "Yes! Of course it's her." Back then she
had often tenderly referred to her "Young Zhou," but I had
never met him. I never would have thought that we'd finally
meet here, of all places. Was this funny or tragic?

I had an intensely strong impulse to open up a storehouse of
treasured memories with the "Young Zhou" of those earlier
days.

"Were you in the Bohai District of Shandong in 1943?" I
challenged him with the first question.

He looked at me uncertainly without acknowledgment one
way or the other, but I seemed to have hit the mark. I went on.
"Did this Wang Lei tell you about the time she nearly starved to
death in the brush?"

At this, he fixed his eyes on me for a full minute, then said,
slightly stunned, "How did you know?" This confirmed that
Wang Lei was indeed his wife.

"How could I not know? I nearly died in there, too. I even ate the chewing gum she was planning to give you!''

Suddenly he studied me with a new degree of interest, increased tenfold. ''She once said that when she had no way out, there was a dog that led the way and saved you all. She said there was a fellow with a Shanghai accent who carried her luggage on his back—was that you?''

''She has a good memory. I was the only one among the nine of us with a Shanghai accent.''

Thus, I became instantly familiar and intimate with the Young Zhou whom I had never met. It was that red thread of Wang Lei's that bound me to him. Young Zhou, by now Old Zhou, was unable to put up his defenses again. And what had broken that dike was the power of love that a young woman brought to him from an enemy-occupied city twenty-six years ago. He reveled in reminiscing about the joys, sorrows, partings, and reunions of their life together during the war. I was equally stirred. In the miserable course of our walk through the brush, Wang Lei had given our small troup much joy and vitality. There, we were starving as we were now, but the hunger had only lasted two or three days, and everyone's morale had remained high throughout; not like now, where there's no end in sight, where the hunger's an evil prank, where we suffer for nothing. Compared to our present situation, the hunger back then in the woods became, ironically, a happy memory. When we were at our wits end, Wang Lei had given everything she had to prolong our lives. Once I had secretly envied Young Zhou as the luckiest man in the world.

We two now had an inexhaustible common language. Happily and lovingly we talked about Wang Lei, and with such a meaningful topic our life of grim starvation grew much more relaxed, and a layer of sweetness was added to our friendship. Together we hoped that Wang Lei would be able to pass safely through the present storm.

Finally, Old Zhou told me his greatest secret. If he hadn't had a great deal of trust in me he never would have breathed a word of it.

VII

It so happened that Zhou had been the vice–secretary general of the Municipal Committee. How had a responsible cadre from a leading party organ become a criminal overnight?

The story goes back to 1962—September—a time when Hangzhou is heavy with the scent of cassia blossoms. The man who headed both the East China Bureau and the Shanghai Municipal Committee went to West Lake to have an audience with Chairman Mao and report on his work.* He took with him his most trusted follower, Zhang Chunqiao, and others, one of whom was Old Zhou, the vice–secretary general of the committee.

After the day's work, an evening friendship dance was held in an exclusive hotel on West Lake. Zhang Chunqiao and Old Zhou were invited to participate; only the head man did not go. This official, the first secretary of Shanghai, was a big man with an exceptionally large nose, so his voice carried well when giving speeches. Behind his back everyone called him ''Big Nose.'' He had always opposed these socials, being of the opinion that it was not in good taste for men and women to mix at dances. So under his rule dancing had been forbidden in Shanghai since 1958.

The star at this dance was Jiang Qing. Of course she was the most animated one there. Old Zhou watched closely from the sidelines as she danced with Zhang Chunqiao in an unusually intimate manner. At first he didn't pay much attention to this, and just enjoyed the singing and dancing and the sights and sounds of spring. Then Jiang Qing and Zhang Chunqiao swung near him and he heard Jiang Qing say to Zhang, ''That Big Nose of yours is really too much! In Shanghai you can't even dance if you want to, but you can come to my place here and dance to your heart's content. . . .''

Old Zhou was boundlessly loyal to the party and deeply trusted the head of the East China Bureau. After their work was

---

*The writer is referring here to Ke Qingshi, who died at the beginning of the Cultural Revolution.

done and they had returned to Shanghai, he gave a factual report to the head man, who immediately turned and reported verbatim to Zhang Chunqiao what the vice–secretary general had told him. When Jiang Qing got back to Shanghai from Hangzhou she found an excuse not to go back to Beijing by saying that she wanted to go to the Peking Opera Troupe to direct "Taking Tiger Mountain by Strategy." Zhang Chunqiao followed her every day like a shadow. He couldn't help but feel a bit guilty, so he revealed to her the "intelligence report" the first secretary had given him. Perfectly calm, without changing color, Jiang Qing pouted her lips. "This is idle gossip. It's bullshit. What are you afraid of? You've got me! Nevertheless, about that guy Zhou, the vice-secretary who specializes in reporting on people, when I get a chance I'll let him know just how tough this old lady can be!" Coinciding with this, over the next few days Old Zhou told the head man about "rumors from below" that Jiang Qing and Zhang Chunqiao didn't really go to the Peking Opera Troupe but instead were quite plainly carrying on together. Old Zhou was concerned about the effect this was having on people below. The head man, on the other hand, was just worried about not having any gifts with which to flatter Jiang Qing, so he immediately passed the word to Zhang Chunqiao to tell her, "In my Shanghai she can rest easy; there won't be any waves."

Because of his two reports on them, Jiang Qing and Zhang Chunqiao looked upon Old Zhou as a thorn in their side, as the "KGB agent" who had broken up their "sweet affair." As soon as the Cultural Revolution began, Zhang Chunqiao usurped authority over the army and government in Shanghai, and the name of vice–secretary general Zhou came right behind Chen and Cao* in the first group of level-one city cadres to be overthrown. While all the other leading cadres of the Municipal Committee

---

*Chen Pixian was first secretary of the Communist Party of Shanghai Municipality in 1965. He disappeared in 1968 after being attacked, was rehabilitated in 1977, and was a member of the Secretariat of the party's Central Committee until 1987, when he became a member of the Central Committee's Central Advisory Commission. See note on p. 66 on Cao Diqiu.

were put in isolation in their own units, Old Zhou alone, through special orders from Zhang, was locked up in the detention center of the Public Security Bureau lest he spread the scandal about Zhang.

What was Old Zhou's crime? For the life of me I couldn't imagine. But from this I became painfully aware of one point—the present "imperial court" was in the hands of treacherous officials, the empress was domineering, there were miscarriages of justice everywhere, and life was intolerable for the people. I should thank Old Zhou. He was the first person to make me realize exactly what rubbish the so-called leadership of the proletariat was!

In twenty days family members would be permitted to bring supplies to us. We were elated when we thought about the glucose and cod liver oil pills that would be sent, and the fact that this was no longer a fantasy, but a reality soon to be realized. It made those twenty days a little brighter and a little easier to get through. The funny thing was that that span of time also seemed to pass so slowly and drearily. Dr. Gu looked after me and Old Zhou with meticulous care, and he was the one to suggest that since he already had two packs of glucose, we could divide a little up among us and pay him back when our own supplies came in. We did just that.

Provisions day finally arrived. Just after 10:00 in the morning, Old Zhou was called out. He received soap, toilet paper, and several scraps of cloth—but no glucose. "I have the doctor's permission," he said. "I have a swollen liver. I already wrote to tell my family. . . ." But the person in charge of family packages impatiently replied, "I know all about that. The procedures don't mean anything. The authorities have notified us it's not allowed in." When Old Zhou came in the door, his face was pale. This was the toughest blow of all. He threw his soap and toilet paper to the floor and broke down. "The authorities, the authorities . . . I know who it is who wants to torment me to death!"

Anxious and fearful, I waited for them to call my number. I was genuinely worried. Could what happened to Old Zhou happen to me, too? At 11:30 they shouted my number. I walked out of the cell, my heart beating wildly. They wouldn't let me see which relative brought my things in, but I did see part of my parcel. My number was written on top, and inside were two packages of glucose that caught my eye. But when the head guard handed me the articles one by one, he put aside the glucose—the glucose I had dreamed about day and night. He looked at me. "The authorities have notified us you can't send in glucose." I was so irritated and angry I thought of grabbing it away, and I nearly wept. "Why isn't it allowed in if the doctor okayed it?" Unmoved, the guard responded coldly, "Don't bother to ask. Next month when your family comes to bring more things, we'll just have them take these two packages home with them, that's all." Then he waved the two bottles of cod liver oil pills under my nose. "You can take these."

I barely had the strength to walk back to the cell. My vision was blurred and I couldn't see anything clearly. My fury rose to the breaking point and I wanted so to shout, "Why in the world not let in medicine from my family? Do you still have human hearts? Even treatment of enemy POWs couldn't be this barbaric!" But who would listen if I really did cry out?

As soon as I rushed into the cell everyone guessed from my expression that I had had bad luck. Old Zhou and I shared the same fate, and I wanted to embrace him and weep. But he comforted me, "Still, you're a little better off than me. They let you have the cod liver oil pills!"

We felt especially guilty about Dr. Gu. We had promised to return to him the glucose we'd taken. How would we repay him now? Weren't we perfect illustrations of the expression, "You can't be a good person in prison?" With no alternative I could only repay him with a bottle of cod liver oil pills. But he absolutely refused to accept it and consoled us, saying that it wasn't our fault we couldn't repay him. Nobody had imagined that even with the doctor's approval the prison supplies center could keep it out. He said we didn't have to pay him back. What especially moved us, though, was what he told Old Zhou. "It's very possible that your swollen liver will develop into hepatitis. If the supplies your family sends aren't permitted in, there's really nothing we can do for you. I still have half a package I'll let you have first. I can have my family send some more in. This stuff is very cheap on the outside. Who would have thought it would be such a treasure here?!''

Old Zhou could tell that Dr. Gu was being sincere and not just offering this out of politeness. But he insisted on refusing the kindness. I offered him a bottle of cod liver oil pills, but it was only after repeated urging on my part that he finally accepted it.

One morning four days later, before Old Zhou had even made it to the squat hole, he began to vomit without stop. Beads of sweat appeared on his forehead as he threw up. Dr. Gu felt his temperature, which seemed close to 106 degrees. He hurried to the door and told the guard to ask for Dr. Wen. The doctor soon arrived, took Old Zhou's blood pressure, looked at the coating on his tongue, and drew blood. Dr. Gu took the opportunity to ask Dr. Wen softly, ''Why were your prescriptions ignored? How come they wouldn't allow in the glucose from his family?''

Wen Dakai assumed a grave expression and lowered his voice. ''It was under special order from Zhang Chunqiao and Ma Tianshui.* There was nothing I could do.''

Ten minutes later two prison workers wearing face masks came in carrying a stretcher. They said 1073 had acute hepatitis and was being sent to the hospital at Tilanqiao Prison. With tears in my eyes I gathered together his quilt and other assorted belongings. A few days ago we had become such close friends, and now we had to part so abruptly—I was inexpressibly sad and bitter. What kind of future could he have in such a terrible place, with such a horrible illness, when the likes of Zhang Chunqiao,

---

*Ma Tianshui was associated with the Shanghai Municipal Revolutionary Committee since its inception in 1967 and served as one of its vice-chairmen and as a secretary of the Shanghai Municipal CCP. In 1976 he came under fire as one of the leading members of the ''Jiang Qing counterrevolutionary clique in Shanghai.''

Jiang Qing, and Ma Tianshui were determined to kill him? I didn't dare imagine.

As I put his pillow on the stretcher I saw the embroidered name "Zhou Xinguo." Old Zhou had cut the scrap of cloth into the shape of a heart and cleverly sewn it to one corner of his pillowcase. This made me think about his loving wife Wang Lei. I had been witness to the creation of this revolutionary household, and now I was viewing the destruction of the same happy home.

As he made his way out, leaning up against the wall for support, I saw that his skin had taken on a greenish tinge. In parting he smiled a little at his cellmates—the wan smile of an oil lamp about to be extinguished. I couldn't bear to look at his face again, afraid that he'd notice my silent weeping. But he had seen it from the beginning, and said softly, "Don't be sad. Take good care of yourself." The iron door shut, ruthlessly separating us.

He was such a good Communist. His crime stemmed from his loyalty to the party.

I couldn't sleep all that night. The bedbugs were besieging me, but I didn't feel up to killing them. I thought about a lot of things, including whether or not the reason my package of glucose hadn't been allowed in was that Zhang Chunqiao, Jiang Qing, Ma Tianshui, and their bunch had wanted me tormented to death, too. I saw the specter of death beckoning me.

VIII

Old Zhou's acute hepatitis terrorized everyone in the cell. Hepatitis was mercilessly contagious, and even more infectious for people already weakened. Because our eating conditions were so abominable, if we really did get sick, all we could do was prepare to die. So everybody felt as if our death sentences had already been passed.

Dr. Gu was clearly aware that he was at the brink of death. Perhaps the hepatitus virus was already incubating inside him. Like us, he displayed a detached attitude, resigning himself to fate. "We lived so closely with 1073—nearly on top of him twenty-four hours a day. At this point, it's too late to think of a way to immunize ourselves against the disease, and anyway, it's impossible to fight it." He spread his hands in a helpless gesture, as if to embrace the god of death.

It wasn't until the afternoon of the next day that we heard that the District Epidemic Prevention Station was going to send people over to disinfect our cell and give everyone a blood test. As the Epidemic Prevention Station personnel all wore masks, we could hardly tell the men from the women. Before their arrival, the guards had walked past our cell door as if nothing had happened, but now they looked nervous. They wore face masks and stood far away lest the germs fly into their noses. The guard in front—the one with the extra piece of flesh under his ear—summoned us loudly in a Yangzhou accent: "Take all your clothes, bedding, and eating utensils to get sterilized."

"Should we take the works of Chairman Mao, too?" asked the cellist in our group.

"How is it you don't call them 'precious books'?" said the guard. "Even the 'precious books' are infected. Of course they go with the rest." But the guard spoke too loudly and was overheard by the commanding officer behind him, who rudely pulled off his face mask. Only then was the guard aware of his indiscretion. His face instantly paled. Begging forgiveness, he slapped his own mouth as hard as he could. "I've committed an offense! I'm a criminal! I blurted it out without thinking. I'll go, I'll go admit my error and ask for punishment. I deserve to die ten thousand deaths!"

The commanding officer did not relax his tightly drawn face. "You ought to know you can't just apologize and forget about this sort of thing," he said sternly. The officer then dragged the guard off somewhere. Thus we witnessed an "active counterrevolutionary" crime from beginning to end. At first, seeing the guard who'd thrown the rotten egg that time get punished made us feel that evil had gotten its just reward, and we gloated over his misfortune. But then I grew depressed. It occurred to me that a large proportion of the more than two thousand prisoners locked up here were probably imprisoned for committing the same error. Wasn't our He Longjiang also an "active counter-revolutionary"? Sure enough, one month after our cell was disinfected, a veteran offender who was transferred in with us mentioned that the guard who'd been on duty here, a guy nicknamed "Young Yangzhou," had been incarcerated with him. Though nobody there knew what he was in for, I suspect it was for running off at the mouth.

After we had cleared our cell, we were led by another masked guard to a room on the second floor so the Epidemic Prevention people could get to work.

"There's only one person in here," the guard warned before opening the cell door. "Don't anyone talk to him. After they're done disinfecting, you're going back down to your own cell."

I was envious that one person was given such a big cell. Compared to our situation, with people piled on top of one another, one person to a cell looked really comfortable and indicative of excessive preferential treatment. But Liu Zhihou and Dr. Gu disagreed with me. "I prefer more people together," said Liu Zhihou. "So what if it's a bit crowded? It's much easier to get by that way. If you're locked up for a long time all alone with no one to talk to for days on end, your mind will become numb and slow and you won't be able to find the words to talk anymore!"

"It's inhumane to lock somebody up alone. Man's a social creature," said Dr. Gu.

Since the guard had already ordered us not to talk with the person in the cell, we deliberately kept our distance from the stranger. He remained on the floor, covered with a woolen blanket. But I grew curious and wanted to walk closer to see what he was like. Was he sick? Why was he in solitary confinement?

I approached him timidly. His bright eyes looked right at me. I reacted with a start, then avoided his gaze. But when our eyes met a second time, I nearly ran over and cried out and threw myself on top of his blanket. It was like a dream—I never imagined I'd meet up with my teacher Xu Yushu here.

But reason had to take control of my bold, wild emotion. I had to maintain the appearance of being a perfect stranger. I approached him quietly. "How did you get here?"

I knew he wasn't working in Shanghai, because we had been corresponding since Liberation. After 1962 he'd been transferred from Beijing to the Southwest to take up a leadership position.

Though he spoke in a very low voice, every word was deeply engraved on my heart. "Before Liberation I was in special charge of organizational work in the party underground in Shanghai. Wang Hongwen, Ye Changming, and their gang of hoodlums were determined to label all underground party comrades part of a traitorous clique. I was their chosen point of penetration—as soon as I admitted to being a traitor, hundreds of Shanghai's underground comrades in the party would be traitors with me. They dragged me back from Guangxi as soon as the movement to purify the ranks began."

It was strenuous for him to talk, but since he didn't know about the order the guard had given when we entered, he had no qualms about speaking to me. Also, having been boxed in here alone year in and year out, he needed someone to whom he could unburden his heart and loosen his stiff tongue. My cellmates were happy for me that I had met up with an old comrade-in-arms, and several of them volunteered to stand at the door to keep watch.

"If I'd really admitted to being a traitor," Teacher Xu went on, "I truly would have become one. This would have been tantamount to selling out hundreds of party comrades. They had braved untold dangers at the hands of the Guomindang reactionaries in those days, risking their heads for the revolution. Now that the revolution had succeeded, how could they become traitors overnight? They sure picked the wrong point of attack in me."

I thought back to our life behind bars more than forty years ago. He was so strongwilled, so solicitous of his fellow prisoners. And then there was the unforgettable episode of the sesame seed biscuit. All of this was evidence of his lofty Bolshevik character.

I noticed scars below his ears and saw that his face was unusually emaciated. If it weren't for the fact that he spoke with such strength and animation, anyone would take him for a man with one foot in the grave.

"Eventually they stopped trying to 'penetrate' the pre-1949 party underground through me. At the beginning, though, they tried to wear me down by rotating my interrogators. Afterward, they used torture. The first week of this month they brought a bunch of thugs who tried four at a time to make me confess. When I wouldn't admit to anything, one of them twisted my head, two grabbed my feet, and they flung me in mid-air, slamming my backbone against the floor. In the old days, when the Guomindang caught me, they used torture too. But the torture used by 'our own people' is somewhat more civilized. They beat you quite meticulously so that no scars or bruises show."

I lifted the blanket covering him. He patted his stomach. "One throw and all my insides shook loose. I've been thrown around like that twice by them and now I can't walk upright. I had to crawl into this cell."

I went nearly mad with rage. I was incapable of explaining how it was that in "our people's" prison they could use such irrational punishment, punishment more barbarous than that of the Guomindang.

"The people who beat me were country youths who'd been in the army only a few days," he continued, faintly. "They were sent out to 'help the left' in order to gain 'frontline training' and 'cultivate feelings for class struggle,' so they said. The sad thing is that these naive kids were deceived into thinking they were 'making revolution'! How could they know they were laying a Communist at death's door?"

It was fortuitous that when gathering up my belongings to be disinfected I had put my most prized possession—the bottle of cod liver oil pills—into my pocket. I swiftly took the bottle out of my pocket and stuck it by his pillow. "What are you giving me?"

"My family just supplied me with half a bottle of cod liver oil pills, but I don't have much use for them. I'm giving them to you. Maybe they'll do you some good.''

But he firmly refused them. ''Seeing you here makes me very happy. I've said more today than I have over the past year. Our meeting isn't accidental, just as our being together forty years ago wasn't either. I don't want you to give me a thing. Your face, too, is yellowish, and your hair has turned white.''

I couldn't help but lie. ''You keep them. I've still got some glucose.''

Only then did he agree to accept the pills.

He put the bottle in his hand and looked at it. ''Old Wang, I don't expect to be in this world much longer. If I die, when you get out you have to report to the party Central Committee that trash like Wang Hongwen must under no circumstances take over the leadership. That group is full of jackals and wolves, murderers and gangsters. And you must bear witness for me. The comrades of Shanghai's party underground are all good people who withstood long trials. When their personal histories were examined during the investigation of all cadres in 1953, each and every one of them came out clean. On my word as a Communist, I guarantee that none of us ever did anything to stain the honor of the party. Any false confessions they fabricate are part of a big conspiracy.''

''I'll remember.'' I clasped his hand tightly. ''I'll be your witness!'' But tears were falling onto my hands, for I had no assurance that I myself would live to get out.

''But I absolutely mustn't die.'' He let out a heavy sigh. ''If I do, a witness is done away with. This group of thugs would forge my handwriting to create false evidence and incriminate my comrades in the party underground. They'd do anything!''

He pulled me closer to his side and signaled me to lower my head. I pressed my ear close to his mouth. ''Please remember, so that in the future you can act effectively as my witness: Anything dated after July 1, 1969, wasn't written by me. I didn't write a word after July 1. Anything they come up with is false. I'm responsible for the political fate of more than four hundred underground members of the party!''

Xu Yushu had overextended himself. Perhaps his face was flushed because of the emotion. I knew this wasn't a good sign, and I was scared. "Do you have anything else to say to your family?" I asked, quietly.

"I have a son in the air force, but because I've been labeled a traitor he can't even serve there. His name is Xu Hongbo. He went back to the Southwest Military District. My wife is with the Grain Bureau in Guangxi. . . . I don't have anything to say. If I say I don't want them implicated because of me, it can't be done, so it would be nothing but empty words. I only ask that they live on staunchly." He stopped for a while, then said, disjointedly, "Have you ever considered that in the enemy's prison I got beriberi and didn't die? Instead, I'll die in a prison of the proletarian dictatorship. Could fate really toy with people like this?"

"My coming here today is also a twist of fate. You're an indestructable diamond. You won't die! From what you've said I can see that you've kept your fighting spirit."

The cellmates keeping watch for me quickly signaled and I stopped talking at once. The iron door opened; we had no choice but to leave.

IX

When we returned to our own cell I couldn't stop thinking about Xu Yushu. What were my sufferings compared to his and Old Zhou's?

About a week later a new prisoner was brought in. His number just happened to be 1296, the same as the elementary school teacher who had killed himself. He was roughly the same age as the teacher. We looked at him with pity, as if he were a reincarnation of the suicide victim, but we couldn't say what we thought. How would he react to the predestined relationship between them? Would he have fatalistic thoughts? Would he, too, take his own life?

To the contrary. He was an optimist, completely indifferent to his so-called crime. He carried himself as if it were an honor to be here. His philosophy was also rather strange. "As soon as I started school I was taught to hate the enemy and to be ice cold and merciless toward him. But nowadays it's gotten to the point where there are enemies in every family. Not only don't the people hate the enemy, but they look upon us as kin.'' With this thinking to sustain him, he would not commit suicide. He carried in a piece of news that grieved everyone. Shanghai's vice-mayor in charge of culture and education had killed himself after being unable to withstand further persecution.

''Is that true? How did he die?'' asked Liu Zhihou.

''The details aren't clear. I just heard that he was locked up someplace with only an old woman around. One morning she got up and found he'd committed suicide.''

Liu Zhihou's face fell. ''He was an expert on international affairs and did many good things for the Communist Party. He was the one who organized the translation and printing of Edgar Snow's *Red Star Over China*.*

''I hear he worked as a translator for the U.S. Information Service, so of course he was considered an American spy,'' added the new inmate.

''Were there any other charges against him?'' asked Liu Zhihou.

''None.''

The vice-mayor's death had nothing to do with himself, so Liu Zhihou felt consoled. He had a clear conscience because from beginning to end he had not provided any information harmful to the now deceased man.

He was silent for a long time. Then, as if making a new discovery, he exclaimed, ''It doesn't look like they'll let me out to enjoy another day of freedom.''

Later facts proved that Liu Zhihou was only half correct, because after the vice-mayor's death there wasn't any point in compelling Liu to divulge any information about the man. Two

---

*The man described here is Jin Zhonghua (1907–68). Jin, never a party member, was an international specialist and journalist who, together with Zou Taofen, started several popular newspapers and periodicals. Jin once worked for the USIS in Shanghai. After 1949, as vice-mayor of Shanghai, he often went abroad on peace missions.

weeks later he obtained an "educational release." He was the only one in our cell to be given such a release.

Political Consultative Conference member Liu Zhihou hadn't been out for more than a few days when Dr. Wen told Dr. Gu from the doorway that 1073 had died from acute hepatitis. Again I was upset for quite a few days. The image of stalwart Old Zhou with his unswerving determination often appeared before me. Sometimes, superimposed over this image was the form of Wang Lei with her loose hair. It made me dizzy; I suspected it was hunger that made my eyes cloud over. In fact, it was the moisture from my tears that produced this picture. Yet because of all the death and suffering I had dealt with, my emotions were not as fragile as before and I was not as easily moved as when I had first arrived. I knew that my tears, laments, and resentment could not be of the slightest help in this perverse and violent world.

The authorities, probably because it was disastrous to have too many people in a cell, issued instructions that a way should be found to clear a group of us out. Or perhaps it was because the reckless charges against me by the two people who had written the big-character poster were indefensible. In any event, after being caged up in this appalling place of terror and cruelty for over six years, I was released at the end of 1974.

The Guomindang reactionaries [in 1934] had sentenced me to ten years, but I was freed after serving only three and a half. I had always rejoiced over my good fortune. Who would have thought that after the revolution succeeded, I'd have to pay off that free time I earned through sheer luck by serving time in a CCP prison? Was this personal destiny or just a tragedy of the times?

No matter; in the end I walked out alive. But there was an invisible yoke around me. It was worse than a real yoke because it made people stay away from me and my friends desert me. It marred my dignity and corroded my soul. They say such a yoke was supposed to reform people's thoughts. This punishment—this yoke—is a product of Eastern civilization and is known as "wearing a cap." Wearing this invisible yoke, I saw the free world and ran toward it. But how could I run? I was on the verge of death when I was released. My legs, thin as twigs, were unable to negotiate the steps of the public bus. I was like a sick person not completely recovered from typhoid. Lice crawled in my collar. Only by bracing myself against the walls lining the streets was I able to get home. I had sworn long ago, like Liu Zhihou, that as soon as I walked out through the prison gate I would eat a bowl of meat noodles. Even though I was limping, I hoped to realize this humble desire. With tremendous effort, I walked into a snack shop. "I want a bowl of braised pork noodles," I called out at the counter. I fished out a few dimes, but I didn't have any grain ration tickets on me. I excused myself, licked my lips, and walked out angrily. The restaurant worker thought I was some refugee from out of town.

Thank heavens in the end I did walk out alive. I discovered that in fact my family and neighbors didn't run away at the sight of me, but looked at me with silent sympathy. This proved that what 1296 had said made sense, that "people don't really hate the enemy, but look upon us as kin." Once something is taken to excess, it will turn about and face the opposite direction. Perhaps this product of Eastern civilization—this "wearing a cap"—was not so effective in the East after all.

Though I was under tight surveillance, when my strength returned I secretly went to search out the relatives of my fellow inmates, as they had asked me to do.

I found the home of Wang Lei first. I'd not been to her house since coming to Shanghai because our jobs were so different and we'd had no contact. Now, here I was entering her home with such horrid news. She lived in a small, dark back room, the kind allotted to someone considered an enemy of the people. It was about fifteen square meters. I hardly recognized her. Shocks and tragedies had so crushed this once brave and lively young woman that she now looked like Xiang Lin's wife from the movie.* Her

---

*Xiang Lin's wife is a character in Lu Xun's short story "The New Year's Sacrifice," which was made into the movie to which the author is referring. She was a wretched country woman who, after being widowed twice and losing her young son to wolves, ages unnaturally quickly and becomes physically decrepit.

eyes were dull and dark. Her once dimpled cheeks were now all wrinkled. When she first saw me she didn't dare acknowledge me, but once she recognized who I was, she gasped. "Is that you? My friend who ate the locusts in the brush?" Her exclamation was so intimate, so sweet, voiced in the same carefree gentle tone from the days when I had known her.

"Where's your son Zhou Xinguo?" I asked.

"How did you know about him?" she replied with surprise. "He's at Xinhai Farm. He's been there for five years now."

"Then how many children do you have here with you?" Afraid of breaking her heart, I purposely didn't mention Old Zhou.

"I also have a daughter, sent down to the countryside in Anhui. We're so bad off now I don't even have a bench for you to sit on."

Forcing back my tears, I asked, "And how is that Young Zhou of yours?"

She paused a moment, her eyes looking blankly out the door. One hand trembled as she pointed to a chest of drawers where a desk clock should sit. "He's over here." I knew long ago that Old Zhou had died, but these three words struck me like lightning. The hair on my body stood on end.

I followed her slightly shaking hand to watch her remove a piece of black cloth from a black wooden urn. I couldn't bear it any longer and choked with sobs. A veteran party member, strong and full of energy, who had struggled all his life, was reduced overnight to nothing but ash. What more was there to say?

I originally had not planned to tell her about the few days Old Zhou and I had together before he died, but when I saw the heart-shaped design of Zhou Xinguo's name sewn on the urn cloth, tears rolled down my face. "This was the heart from his pillowcase, wasn't it?"

Wang Lei suddenly looked at me wide-eyed.

"It came from your son's pants, didn't it?"

I had asked only two simple questions, but she grew more and more puzzled, so I told her straight out how Old Zhou and I had been locked up together, how I'd watched him get sick, how I saw him apply to allow his family to send him glucose, which the guard wouldn't let in, how I watched his acute hepatitis flare up, and how we had bid our final farewell.

Wang Lei lay across the table sobbing. Then she lifted her head and gazed at me long and meaningfully. The rims of her eyes were deep red. Her stare made me uneasy. "You are truly fine," she said softly. "That you could live closely with him the last days of his life means he couldn't have felt lonely before he died. Even as his wife, I was unable to see him then, even once. I was isolated in an underground room with no light, living a life of fear and terror. I thought of my children, of Old Zhou, of my mother. I thought about what our country would do from now on. They insisted I was a traitor. I told them I hadn't been involved in the revolution until I'd gone to the base areas, and I had never been caught by the Guomindang or Japanese devils, so how could I be a traitor? They said that I breathed the same air as Old Zhou, so I must be a traitor. No wonder there are traitors everywhere, when everyone who participated in the revolution has become one. I was locked up there a year and nine months. I never saw any sunlight. Sometimes I was fed, sometimes not. My depression from all that left me completely bald when I got out."

Wang Lei smoothed over her few strands of hair.

"Only my daughter was here when I got home. Zhou Xinguo had already been sent off to Xinhai Farm. The first thing I saw when I walked in the door was this urn. At first I didn't know what was inside it. I asked my daughter. 'Daddy's inside it!' she replied. How could it be? I threw myself onto the urn and read the line of white writing that had his name and date of death. Only then did I clutch it and weep."

"Then when the scraps of cloth and the glucose were sent in, you weren't at home?"

"That was my daughter's doing. She was only fifteen then. She managed the house all by herself without either of her parents. She wanted to tell her father that her brother Zhou Xinguo had been sent to Xinhai Farm. She knew she couldn't write to him, so she found that pair of pants her brother had worn when he was little. She thought her father would understand everything when he saw the embroidered name.''

Wang Lei pulled out two packages of glucose wrapped in plastic from the bottom of a net bag. I felt them with my hand. The glucose had already hardened. Tears rolled down my face. ''He died suffering so,'' she said. ''He wasn't even able to take two spoonfuls of glucose. It wasn't easy for our daughter to save the money to buy it, and then after she sent it in they wouldn't accept it. She had to bring it back. On the anniversary of his death we used these two packages as an offering to him. Since he couldn't take it while he was alive, the least we could do was let him see it now that he was dead!''

I placed the brick-hard packages before Old Zhou's urn as an offering and began to cry again as I faced his remains. But Wang Lei soberly urged me not to cry because it might alarm the neighbors. ''We're a black household!'' she said, lowering her voice.

I immediately restrained my tears and stiffened up, as if I had done something wrong. Just then a young high school student walked in the door. She looked exactly like her mother. This young girl noted right off that my eyes were wet and, walking over to her mother, said in a soft voice, ''It must be an old comrade-in-arms of Daddy's.''

''You must call him Uncle Wang,'' said Wang Lei.

Her daughter bashfully addressed me as Uncle Wang.

''What's your name?'' I asked. ''Have you been assigned work yet since graduation from high school?'' I figured she was close to twenty, the age when one is assigned a job.

''Her name is Wang Bao,'' answered her mother. ''She graduated from high school last year. They could care less whether I had any children at home. They said that since her father was a counterrevolutionary, his offspring would certainly have to go down to the countryside and undergo reeducation. She went to Anhui and before a year was up returned as skinny as a rag picker. On top of all this I was in a sickly state, so when she came home at Chinese New Year I didn't let her go back. If she left, how could an old woman like me get by all alone keeping watch over an urn?''

I had told her everything; there was nothing more to say. I knew that whatever I said would be of no use. Wang Bao's presence in this gloomy room the size of my palm was like a ray of brilliant sunlight shining on us. Not only did she have her mother's beauty when she was young, she also had a slight melancholy in her eyes, and that kind of mature and steady demeanor that examines the world around it with extreme vigilance. She exuded a sedate, well-balanced, maidenly beauty that made her stand out from other people, and I was very happy for Old Zhou that he had such a lovely daughter.

"Is it all right if she doesn't go to the countryside?" I asked.

"They've already taken my husband and son. I won't let them take my daughter too. Of course, I know that from now on she'll be an unregistered person without legal residence here."

"Why is her last name Wang instead of Zhou?"

"To draw a clear distinction between herself and her counter-revolutionary father. They say if she keeps her father's surname, in the future she'll face problems, even difficulty finding a spouse. But what actually happened? Even though she changed her name, she wasn't able to escape adversity. She was still sent to a remote farm village, and they made her write reports on her ideology when she got to the production brigade."

My heart was as heavy as lead. I'd planned to give Wang Lei some spiritual encouragement and comfort, but I had completely forgotten about this important mission. What could I do to comfort the widow and the fatherless child before me?

"When did you get out?" asked Wang Lei.

"I was much more fortunate than Old Zhou, all things considered. I came out alive. Everything is fine with me now."

When her daughter realized I'd been with her father before his death, she broke in, "How did they kill my father?"

"Your father developed acute hepatitis and was sent to the Tilanqiao Prison Hospital. He died there."

She glanced at me with distrust for a moment, then said decisively, "No, that's not right. My father's health was so good that when he went in he even said to me, 'Don't cry, Xiao Bao, I'll be back in a few days.' Then out of the blue they notified me to pick up his ashes. I don't believe Daddy could have died. How could he have died if they didn't kill him?"

Her eyes burned with hatred, and her voice was searing and determined. I could only admit that her judgment was correct, and that I had given her a surface response not based on reality. "You're right. Your father really *was* killed by them," I hurriedly declared. "And what's more, I know who his murderers are."

"Where is this killer? What's his name?" Wang Bao was unable to restrain herself.

"They're on top of a pyramid. How are you going to get at them?"

Her eyes shone fiercely for a moment. "A pyramid . . . you mean a pyramid in Egypt? If the murderer has run away to Egypt, I'll arrest him and bring him back." She was so serious and so determined that I regretted using this playful metaphor.

"Come on, who is it? Tell me, okay?" she implored.

"I'll tell you when you're a little older."

She pursed her lips in dissatisfaction, then asked, "Uncle Wang, what do you do?"

I gave a start. It was best to answer vaguely. "I'm a teacher by negative example."

The young girl didn't understand what I meant. "Are you a teacher in middle school?"

"Yes. I teach physical education. I'm a veteran athlete."

I smiled at her childish, lovable face. Her mother, knowing what I meant, smiled — but it was a bitter smile.*

There remained only one thing to say. "Live staunchly on. Believe in the party, believe in the people, and believe that the sky above us will one day be bright."

---

*The word for "athlete" in Chinese is *yundongyuan,* or "movement person." Thus a veteran athlete is a pun for someone who has been through many political movements.

X

After that I went to Dr. Gu's home. He'd had four large rooms, but only two were left to him during the current assault—quite a lot of space compared to what Wang Lei had. I visited his home at night. When his wife saw a stranger rush in, her face turned completely white. "Who are you looking for?" she asked quickly. I answered softly from the door. "Dr. Zhu Yanyun [Dr. Gu's wife]." She continued watching me while leading me into the house. I wanted to dispel her doubts quickly, so I introduced myself as soon as we were in the room. "I was imprisoned with Dr. Gu."

This erased her misgivings, razed the barrier between us, and won her trust. She motioned me to sit on the sofa, which must have been badly worn because a large towel had been laid over it. I noticed her hair was spotted with white, and she wore a pair of gold-rimmed glasses. Her face was thin and pallid. She looked depressed. Welcoming this unexpected guest to her home made her relax a bit. She asked eagerly, "Is he all right in there?"

"Not bad. Every day he thinks of you, and he never stops worrying." That's all I could reply.

Her eyes welled up with tears at once. "I'm just fine. What good does it do for him to worry about me? I only pray that he stays alive."

"He asked me to tell you that he wants you to send a report to Chairman Mao on his behalf. Write down the injustices of his case. A single word from the old man will win his release."

Zhu Yanyun hesitated a moment. "I wrote reports to Chairman Mao *and* to Premier Zhou to no avail; my letters might as well have been stones sinking into the sea. In China there's nothing you can do." Then she related to me the real story of her husband's so-called crime. Jiang Qing and Wang Hongwen wanted to get the credit for discovering acupuncture anesthesia and use it as political capital, as an achievement exemplifying their good government. They wouldn't allow anyone else to assume the inventor's rights, but as Dr. Gu didn't understand the inside story, a year earlier he had told an overseas Chinese doctor about the finding. Thus he had committed the serious crime of divulging state secrets. Three years ago the New China News Agency publicly announced to the world the success of acupuncture anesthesia in surgical operations. Among other things it mentioned that this was yet another of the rich successes of the Great Proletarian Cultural Revolution. Of course they couldn't trace the achievement to any one doctor. No one would ever have imagined that the doctor who had first experimented with acupuncture anesthesia was imprisoned, and for so long.

It was apparent that this pharmaceutical specialist had a lot of political judgment and her own point of view. Even though she spoke very calmly, I discerned hatred and rage in every word. "I figured that since New China News Agency had already published the news, the charge of divulging state secrets would no longer hold water, so once the news was publicized I wrote to Premier Zhou asking that he rescue Dr. Gu. I waited and worried day in and day out, but in the end there was no action. Old Gu has been locked up there all this time."

"The problem was that your letters couldn't reach Chairman Mao or Premier Zhou because of all the obstacles along the way. I heard that Premier Zhou became ill and went into the hospital. He was probably even less likely to see letters there."

This seemed to remind her of something. Pausing for a minute to think, she said, "Yes, that's one way. The premier is in the hospital. I know people in several of the hospitals in Beijing."

In the summer of 1975 Dr. Gu was finally released. I went to his home to congratulate him. Only then did I find out, from Zhu Yanyun, that right after my visit that night she had made inquiries and discovered that the Central Committee had asked Shanghai to recommend several well-known surgeons to go to Beijing to treat the premier. Among them was a classmate of Dr. Gu's who had studied in America with him. She asked him personally to deliver her letter into the premier's hands. During his illness Premier Zhou had personally concerned himself with the matter.

Finally Dr. Gu was released by order from Vice-Premier Deng Xiaoping.

Before long, Deng was again overthrown.* Zhu Yanyun found a way to come see me. Her face was pale and her voice was shaking. "It looks like Dr. Gu will be locked up again. Big-character posters about him have been put up again at school, saying that he's a 'resurrected recluse' whom Deng Xiaoping sprung from prison."†

Her anxiety was justified. She thought I could figure a way out of this disaster, but what answers did I have for her? I was hardly able to save myself, let alone anyone else!

Tears appeared on her face when she realized I had no solution. "Premier Zhou *would* have to die just now. If the old man goes in again, I'm afraid he won't come out alive."

"He's very tough," I could only comfort her hollowly. "He won't die. He shouldn't even think of dying. But still, don't forget to send in glucose . . . or find a way for him to go away somewhere and lie low until this thing blows over." Dr. Zhu left.

After the fall of the "Gang of Four," Dr. Gu was safe and sound. It turned out he had taken my advice and gone to Xinjiang Military Hospital to hide out for six months.

Still wearing my invisible "label," I hurried to Dr. Zhu Yanyun's home. Right off, Dr. Gu embraced me and kissed me emotionally, the way Westerners do. He cried tears of happiness. His face was rosy and the traces of worry had disappeared. "We lived through it! Our days as prisoners and fugitives are over at last!" He was overjoyed.

Dr. Zhu ceremoniously served me, this "starving devil,"

---

*The resilient Deng Xiaoping was purged in 1966, rehabilitated in 1973–74, overthrown again in 1976 (the time to which the author is referring here), and brought back into the leadership in 1977.

†The Chinese term for "resurrected recluse," *ju yimin*, was used at the time in a derogatory fashion to describe those learned or skilled intellectuals labeled "bad elements" who, after a period of incarceration, were freed by Deng Xiaoping and his followers and allowed to resume their original positions and professions.

Western food she had prepared herself, saying to her husband, "It was only because of his suggestion that I got you to Xinjiang."

Dr. Gu and I toasted each other. Smiling, he said, "I want to thank you very much for the other lousy idea you came up with for her to continue sending me glucose. Right?"

"Right! How could I forget to repay your glucose? I plan to add interest to it a hundred times over."

Thus we raised our glasses to celebrate the great victory of the smashing of the "Gang of Four."

The house had been redecorated. Cassia flowers and several branches of amaranths stood in a large glass vase.

I was sure Xu Yushu was no longer alive. After the fall of the "Gang of Four," I wrote a letter to his wife in Nanning asking what had happened to him. Her reply made me rejoice. He hadn't died after all! This invincible, unconquerable, immortal warrior had lived through it. It was wonderful that he could see the iniquitous "Gang of Four" fall from power. His wife wrote that he had just been released from prison and had been taken to Huashan Hospital. I rushed over to the third-floor ward of Huashan and there he was, still covered with a blanket, his pale hands resting outside. He sat up excitedly and embraced me. I was unable to speak. He couldn't stop slapping my back. The two of us practically shouted out the same thing, "It's wonderful I've lived to see you."

He was so excited his eyes brimmed with tears. He was gasping for breath. "I must be dreaming. Our victory, the end of the 'Gang of Four,' is more perfect than anything we dreamed!"

I tightly clasped his bony hand. "I still haven't forgotten the task you asked of me on your deathbed. But now there's no need for me to serve as witness, is there?"

He laughed. "We count as historical witnesses to the plot of those counterrevolutionaries—Lin Biao and the 'Gang of Four.' "

"You ought to say we're the gravediggers of the counter-revolutionary sinister clique of Lin Biao and the 'Gang of Four'!"

We talked to our hearts' content about our bitter experiences and Comrade Hua Guofeng's great victory over the "Gang of

Four.'' I found out that Xu had many illnesses: a defective heart, a punctured kidney, blood in his urine; two ribs had caved in where that gang of thugs had walked over his chest with leather shoes. He spoke in short breaths, and his breathing grew rapid when he was excited. He still remembered that half bottle of cod liver oil pills. ''They were like manna from heaven!''

''And I will never forget that sesame biscuit that was such a lifesaver,'' I replied. The two of us laughed freely and embraced once again.

''As long as I live to see the destruction of those rotten eggs, I'll be satisfied. How sad that those who died before us were unable to see that there would be a day such as today!'' He talked about all the things he wanted to do once he was better—construct a hydroelectric power station at the Three Gorges, develop underground mineral resources in Guangxi. . . .

During visiting hours in the afternoon, old comrades from Shanghai's party underground came one after another to call on him, to congratulate him, thank him, and comfort him. Realizing he was being disturbed too much, I left a bit early.

Within the month I took my son to visit him. In the hospital I met his son, who'd been the air force pilot, and I also met Mr. Xu's elderly wife.

Seeing Xu Yushu this time frightened me. His face had become a bit deformed, the blue veins at his temples were twitching slightly, and his voice had weakened. Next to his bed was a wooden rack from which hung a glucose bottle with a rubber tube leading to his arm. Only then did it hit me how feeble he'd become. He was on his way downhill. (Deep in my heart I knew he probably wasn't far from death, but I did my best to get rid of this unlucky thought.) I nestled my head against his breast and listened to his words, spoken with all the strength he had. ''Probably before long I will be going to meet Marx. Examining my life, I don't think I've lived in vain. I'll be going to see Marx with a clear conscience . . . except that I'm unable to face the party because in 1957 and 1958 I mistook more than ten high-level intellectuals for rightists, when really they were all talented people working for the nation. . . . We didn't prevent the rise of the 'Gang of Four' earlier because we didn't use our heads; we blindly believed in the 'highest directive' [Mao Zedong]. This is a disgrace for a Communist Party member. Because of my blindness, I treated my own comrades as enemies. It was like shooting an arrow at the enemy only to have it come back at you. We were punished for this. I was luckier than Comrade Zhang Yunqing.* He didn't live to see the fall of the 'Gang of Four.' I can die without regrets because I have lived to see today. Looking back now, it seems that the construction of the "third front" in those early years violated economic principles and created great waste.† We should transfer our energy to developing our underground natural resources . . . I've already reported this to Vice-Premier Li. . . . '' I couldn't hear the rest at all. He was gasping for breath. It was too much of an effort for him to talk. I couldn't bear to let him continue expending his energy, so I wouldn't let him go on. I held his hand tightly. For the rest of my life I will remember the last words I heard him speak, for "on the verge of death, a man clears his conscience."

On September 20, 1977, the sad news of Xu Yushu's death reached me. I hurried to the hospital. He was quietly resting in the mortuary. He could have done a great many more things for the party, but during those ghastly years his health had been ruined from the inside out. He lived to see the demise of the "Gang of Four" because of his fighting determination and his optimistic spirit. I didn't cry when I paid my last respects to him. I said to myself, "Teacher Xu, may you rest in peace, for you died without regrets."

Draft completed September 1979 at Zhuzhou

---

*Zhang Yunqing is the name Cao Diqiu used in prison.

†The "third front" refers to China's inland areas to which the population retreated in wartime. In the early 1960s the government began to shift China's industrial base to the inner provinces and mountainous areas to protect it from possible nuclear attack and to develop these less developed regions. The policy was later considered unsuccessful, as it was based on irrational planning.

About the Translator

Kyna Rubin, who received her M.A. in Modern Chinese Literature from the University of British Columbia, was among the first students in 1979–80 to conduct research in China for the Committee for Scholarly Communications for the People's Republic of China. She was a professional associate at the CSCPRC from 1982 to 1989 and is now a writer and editor at The Urban Institute. She has worked closely with Wang Ruowang since 1980.